Learning to Love
OTHERS

Book Three

The Learning to Love Series

Small Group Bible Study on
Living the Christian Faith

by Richard Peace

NAVPRESS
BRINGING TRUTH TO LIFE
NavPress Publishing Group
P.O. Box 35001, Colorado Springs, Colorado 80935

Pilgrimage Publishing, Hamilton, Massachusetts

This book is based on an earlier book by the author: *Learning to Love: Book Three. Learning to Love Others*, ©1968 published by Zondervan Publishing House and InterVarsity Press. It has been substantially revised and expanded from the earlier edition and its format and focus have been altered.

ISBN 08910-98402

Cover illustration: Bob Fuller Creative

4 5 6 7 8 9 10 11 12 13 14 15 16 17/99 98 97 96

To Judith,
of course,
once again

————————

The LEARNING TO LOVE series:

Book One: Learning to Love God
Book Two: Learning to Love Ourselves
Book Three: Learning to Love Others

The aim of any Bible study ought to be to bring the reader into contact with Scripture in such a way that his or her life will be changed. This is my aim in *LEARNING TO LOVE.* The focus, therefore, is not on learning doctrine but on learning how to live like a Christian. Doctrine is present, of course, but always in relationship to life.

These studies were written originally in the 1960s to serve as follow-up literature in evangelistic missions conducted by African Enterprise, a group which I helped start while a student at Fuller Theological Seminary and with which I served for eight years in Africa. In their original form, they were published by two presses: Zondervan Publishing House and InterVarsity Press. They went through over twenty editions and were translated into Chinese, Spanish, Portuguese, and Korean. Certain parts of the series were translated into Zulu and Sotho.

But the original *LEARNING TO LOVE* has been out of print for many years. However, I kept getting requests for the books since it seems that nothing quite replaced them. The need remained to assist new Christians in beginning their lives as followers of Jesus. So it seemed appropriate to revise and update *LEARNING TO LOVE* as the inaugural volumes for our new publishing house: Pilgrimage Publishing.

When I first conceived of this project, what I had in mind was a modest updating of the original books coupled with translation from individual studies into a small group format. Of course, as I started working on the project it soon became evident that what was demanded was a thorough-going revision. The result is that only a small part of the original material remains. Most of the original topics are still addressed, generally using the same passages from the Bible, however in different ways. In addition, six new Bible studies have been written (expanding the series from fifteen to twenty-one studies). The result is, I hope, a highly usable series for a new generation of Christians.

The first set of *LEARNING TO LOVE* books was written in South Africa. It is appropriate that the new series was also written in South Africa during my sabbatical from Gordon-Conwell Theological Seminary. I am grateful to the many people who assisted me in completing this new series, both directly and indirectly, especially all the folk on Morningside Farm in Winterton, Natal, South Africa, where I lived while writing. Specifically, I want to thank:

- ◆ Joan Reeve, who opened her farm to my family, giving us a wonderful place to live, and her father Cyril Gemmel, who always had a ready story or comment;
- ◆ all the people who worked on the farm and helped us in one way or another: Musa, Gertrude, Rosie, Mavis, and the rest of the Zulu staff;
- ◆ the young people living and working there: David, Jolyn, and Katelyn Reeve; Bass; Rob Mark; Joel Howe; Jenny and Jonathan Peace; and
- ◆ the unforgettable kids: Daisy and the three musketeers—Sbusiso, Thabani, and Phumleni; as well as the other kids: Sindi, Thokozani, Zanele, and Freedom.

I appreciate the generosity of the Trustees of Gordon-Conwell in giving me the time to write through the sabbatical program. And, of course, my biggest thanks go to my wife Judy, who has supported me through yet another writing project. "Keep it simple. Keep it useful," she kept saying. I hope I did.

Grateful acknowledgment is made to the following publishers for permission to reprint copyright material:

◆ *The Art of Loving* by Erich Fromm (New York: Harper & Row, 1962).

◆ *God's New Society: The Message of Ephesians* by John R. W. Stott (Downers Grove, IL: InterVarsity, 1979).

◆ *The Letter to the Romans (The Daily Study Bible),* translated and interpreted by William Barclay (Philadelphia: The Westminster Press, 1958).

◆ *You Can Witness With Confidence* by Rosalind Rinker (Grand Rapids: Zondervan Publishing House, 1962, 1969).

◆ *Know Why You Believe* by Paul E. Little (Downers Grove, IL: InterVarsity, 1969).

◆ *The Letters of James and Peter (The Daily Study Bible),* translated and interpreted by William Barclay (Philadelphia: The Westminster Press, 1958, 1960).

◆ *The Company of the Committed* by Elton Trueblood (New York: Harper & Row, 1961).

BIBLE VERSIONS

◆ *The New International Version:*
Scripture taken from the *HOLY BIBLE, NEW INTERNATIONAL VERSION.* Copyright ©1973, 1978, 1984 International Bible Society. Used by permission of Zondervan Bible Publishers.

◆ *The Revised Standard Version,* ©1946, 1952, 1971, 1973 by the National Council of Churches of Christ (New York).

Richard V. Peace

An Introduction to the Series

Becoming a Christian is an awesome step to take. In deciding to follow Jesus we are turning our backs on many of the attitudes, actions, and ideas that once guided our lives. We are turning toward the way of life shown us by Jesus. We turn to Christ because we discover that the "old way" was the way of death; Jesus offers the way of life.

In coming to Christ, we are often thrown off balance. It is like living in a fog and having a new and powerful light burst through to show us a completely new path to follow. This can be a disconcerting experience. We no longer know what to make of our old lives; we only barely grasp what this new life holds.

This brings us to the point of this series: its aim is to illuminate the new way of Jesus while helping us to reflect on our old life.

We will examine the key ideas of Christ's way: he gives us a new way of viewing the world around us—a way filled with hope and purpose. We will reflect on the new attitudes that characterize the new way, since Christ helps us to form a new affection. This changes how we view others and what we give ourselves to. Finally, we will examine the kind of lifestyle Jesus wants us to have: what we do matters, and (at times) Christ calls us to stand against the stream of culture.

We will do all this together with others—with some people who have been "on the way" for a while, and others who are just starting on the way. The Christian way was never meant to be a solitary path. The church is intended to be the joyous community of pilgrims aiding and supporting one another "on the way."

A word about how this course has been organized. The three books of this series are structured around the Great Commandment given by Jesus: "Love the Lord your God with all your heart and with all your soul and with all your mind and with all your strength.... Love your neighbor as yourself. "

In Book One, we will look at what it means to learn to love God. God is alive and personal, as present as our next breath. Yet God is also Spirit. Therefore, having a relationship with God is different from having a relationship with another person. We need to consider how one grows and nurtures a relationship with the living God.

In Book Two, we shift the topic from God to ourselves. We ask the question: What does it mean to love ourselves? This is a concept fraught with difficulties. Improper self-love translates into a lifestyle that is hedonistic, selfish, and self-destructive. But we dare not avoid the subject, because failing to love ourselves properly is also self-destructive. With low (or no) self-esteem, people become doormats for others, fail to use their Christ-given gifts, and have difficulty loving others. Jesus calls us to walk the narrow road between selfishness and selflessness. This involves a proper self-understanding, a larger dose of humility, and a healthy sense of who we are.

In the final book, we look at our relationship with other people. Christ's call is, at its root, a call to love others. Yet this is so often difficult. For one thing, others are not always very lovable; for another, loving them sometimes gets in the way of our self-interest. But we cannot avoid the issue. To follow Christ is to live a certain way. Behavior counts; lifestyle matters. But it's not all sacrifice and pain.

Our greatest joys come from others. To be in a loving relationship with other people is to be alive and joyful.

A word to those who are not beginners on the way of Jesus:

So far, it would appear that these studies were written solely for the benefit of those who are new in the faith. In fact, they were written primarily for that purpose. But it's also true that those who have been on the way for some time need to be reminded of the fundamentals of the faith. Martin Luther stressed this to the clergy. He warned them against thinking that once they mastered the catechism (the statement of the fundamentals of the faith), they could then move beyond it. Instead, he urged them to recite the catechism daily as a spiritual discipline. He wrote:

> "As for myself, let me say that I, too, am a doctor and a preacher—yes, and as learned and experienced as any of those who act so high and mighty. Yet I do as a child who is being taught the Catechism.... I must still read and study the Catechism daily, yet I cannot master it as I wish, but must remain a child and pupil of the Catechism, and I do it gladly."[1]

There is something very powerful about remembering what lies at the heart of the faith. As Luther indicates, we can never master even the most fundamental facts. We need to be brought back to them constantly. In a real sense, we never get beyond the ABC's of the faith—nor should we. Thus, this series will be of value to the experienced Christian.

It is useful to have a study group that consists of both new and experienced Christians. Both benefit from the presence of the other. Both need each other in considering what it means to "learn to love." The older Christian brings experience and knowledge—years of seeking to know and live the faith, and this enriches new Christians. On the other hand, the new Christian brings freshness and wonder to this task—new eyes to see old facts in fresh ways, and so those who are older in the faith are reminded why they started on this journey in the first place.

Blessings on you as you seek to walk faithfully on the path to new life in Christ.

---

[1] Theodore G. Tappert, ed. and trans., *The Book of Concord* (Philadelphia: Fortress Press, 1959), page 359, quoted in Robin Maas and Gabriel O'Donnell, *Spiritual Traditions for the Contemporary Church* (Nashville: Abingdon Press, 1990), pages 167–168.

A Three-Part Program

There are three main sections to each chapter. Each section has a special function in the process of learning how to follow Jesus. Knowing the intention of each section will help you use that section to its full advantage:

◆ *Group Study:* contains materials for a 60- to 90-minute small group Bible study.

◆ *Study Resources:* contains notes and comments used in both group and personal study.

◆ *Personal Study:* contains a series of reflection questions for use by group members on their own during the week.

In turn, each of these three sections has various parts, which are discussed below.

Group Study

Small group Bible study is at the heart of this material. This is where you will learn, share, pray, laugh, cry, reflect, and grow—together with a small group of friends and fellow pilgrims. The Christian way was never meant to be a solitary way. It has always been a matter of community. The early Christian groups were not much larger than your small group. They met in homes, studying and worshiping together. It was not until the third century that special buildings were used for the gathering of Christians. So, in forming this small group, you are returning to the original way in which men and women learned to be disciples of Jesus.

Your small group study has several components:

❒ *Overview:* The first page of each chapter has a brief description of the topic to be studied and the materials that are presented in each of the three sections. This will give you a clear idea of what to expect and how to proceed. You will also know what results to strive for as a small group and in your personal study.

❒ *Beginning:* Each small group study will begin with a sharing exercise that puts you in touch with the issue that will be studied. This is a good way to begin a small group because it gets everyone talking. It helps to move you from what you were thinking about (or worried about) when you arrived at the meeting to what the text deals with. It also puts you in touch with the topic in an experiential way, so that your discussion is not just sharing ideas, but sharing your life. Most importantly, it allows you to share your stories with one another. The questions in this section always focus on life experiences, and they are generally fun to answer.

❒ *The Text:* The aim of the entire small group experience is to understand and apply a passage from the Bible to your life. You will study material from various parts of the Bible. Different translations will be used, so that you will become acquainted with the excellent variety of English language Bibles available today. Since the New Testament was written to be read aloud, you will begin your study by reading the text aloud. Words in bold type are explained in the *Bible Study Notes* section.

❏ *Understanding the Text:* Unless you notice carefully what the text says, you will not be able to interpret it accurately. The questions in this section are designed to help you focus on the key issues and assertions in the passage. You will also begin to wrestle with the meaning of the text. In this section, you concentrate on the passage in its original first-century context (in the case of New Testament passages). After someone in the group has read the passage aloud, take five minutes for silent study (in which you think about the answer to each question). The rest of the time is used for small group discussion based on the questions. Optional questions are provided for you to discuss as a group (when time permits), or for you to do as homework.

❏ *Applying the Text:* It is not enough to simply understand the passage. You need to apply that understanding to your own situation. This is the aim of the final section of the small group study. The questions in this section connect what you have read to how you should live.

Study Resources

The *LEARNING TO LOVE* series is enriched by various study resources that extend and expand both the small group study and your own personal study. Some groups will assign certain sections as homework to be completed in preparation for next week's small group. Other groups will assign these as follow-up materials to deepen the small group discussion. In all cases, maximum learning will occur if you take time each week to work through this material.

❏ *Bible Study Notes:* Assisting you in the study of the Bible is a series of notes that will give you the kind of information you need to make sense of the text: definitions of words, comments about cultural practices, background information from other books in the Bible, etc. In addition, each set of notes begins with some comments on how the passage you are studying fits into the unfolding argument or story in the book of the Bible where it is found (Setting). You will find entries in this section for those words and phrases in the text that are printed in bold type. The hope is that these comments will help to bring the text alive.

❏ *Comment:* This is a reflection on the meaning of the text. A key idea in the text will be highlighted, or there will be additional information about some aspect of the text. Sometimes connections are made between the text and your personal circumstances. This section is usually written by the author of the small group study; it may also include selections from the writings of other Christian authors.

Personal Study

❏ *The Art of Bible Study:* In each chapter, one particular aspect of the process of Bible study will be highlighted. The hope is that over the course of the twenty-one studies, you will become a proficient Bible student, able to understand and apply the text on your own. In *Learning to Love God,* the process of observation will be discussed. In *Learning to Love Ourselves,* the process of interpretation will be the focus. And in *Learning to Love Others,* the process of application will be highlighted.

❐ *Extra Reading:* Exploring the world of faith is exciting. It will lead you in many directions. The hope is that these studies will pinpoint the key issues involved in learning to live a life of faith. However, the studies can only introduce various topics. You may find that certain issues interest you, and you will want to explore these in more depth. The books listed here will guide your further exploration. Of course, you will not be able to read all the books listed; however, you should try to read some of them.

❐ *Reflection Questions:* Based on the text you have studied, certain questions will be asked to guide your personal reflections in this section. It is best used as a way to respond on a personal level to the insights that emerged in the small group study. Generally, there is no "right answer" to these questions— only the answer that expresses your own thoughts, feelings, and experience. Sometimes your response will be brief; other times it will be extensive.

❐ *Journal:* The process of journaling is a helpful exercise that promotes spiritual growth. You may not have enough room on this page for all of your thoughts, so you will probably have to let your writing flow over into another journal. In fact, you may want to put all of your reflections in a private journal (so you can freely express what you are thinking and feeling), and use this section to jot down notes about things to share with the group next week.

The Appendix

❐ *The Art of Leadership: Brief Reflections on How to Lead a Small Group:* Almost anyone can lead this small group Bible study successfully—provided they have some sense of how small groups operate and what the function of the small group leader is. This is the aim of this section. It provides a brief overview of how to lead the *LEARNING TO LOVE* small group.

❐ *Small Group Leader's Guide: Notes on Each Session:* In this section, detailed information is given for each small group session. The small group leader should review this material in preparation for each session.

Questions About the Study Guide

Since this book is not designed to be read by an individual on his or her own, but as a guide for small group and personal study, it is important to explain how it is intended to be used. The following questions will give some idea about the various possibilities that exist for this material.

Who is this material designed for?
▶ New Christians who want to learn what it means to follow Jesus as his disciple
▶ All Christians who want to review the fundamentals of the faith
▶ Interested seekers who want to explore the Christian way

What is it about?
▶ What is involved in being a follower of Jesus:
  • How one meets and knows God
  • The spiritual disciplines of Bible study, prayer, and worship
  • What it means to be a spiritual pilgrim, walking in the way of God
▶ Growing and nurturing the Christian life

What are the distinctive features of this series?
▶ These are spelled out in *What It's All About: An Introduction to the Series* and in *How It Works: A Three-Part Program.*

How do I form a group?
▶ Invite a group of (up to) twelve people to your house.
▶ Start with a potluck supper.
▶ After supper, explain the nature of the course.
▶ Give a study guide to each person.
▶ Then do the first session together.
▶ Agree to meet together for six more sessions.

Why should I belong to a group?
▶ It will help you to mature in your Christian life.
▶ Everyone needs the support of others in growing spiritually.
▶ This is a great way to get to know others who are on your wavelength in taking the spiritual side of life seriously.
▶ It's fun!

What if I don't know much about the Bible?
▶ This is the purpose of the small group: to learn more about the Bible together.
▶ The *Bible Study Notes* will increase your understanding of the Bible.
▶ The *Art of Bible Study* will help you to learn how to study the Bible.
▶ In any case, this is a small group for learners (not experts).

Can a church run these sessions?
▶ Sure! This material can be used in many different ways:
  • with new Christians   • in a new members' class
  • in a Sunday school class   • at a weekend retreat
  • in one-on-one discipling
▶ Either the church staff or lay leadership can organize it.

How often should we meet?
- ▶ Once a week is best.
- ▶ Once every other week works well, too.
- ▶ Do all the sessions at two consecutive Saturday seminars (9:00 a.m.–1:00 p.m.).
- ▶ Or do all seven sessions at a weekend retreat.

How long should we meet?
- ▶ You need at least an hour per session.
- ▶ Ninety minutes is best—this gives time for more discussion.
- ▶ Some groups may want to meet for two hours:
  - This would allow more time for sharing.
  - Members could share from their *Journal* reflections.
  - You could also give time for personal study.
  - You could work through the *Study Resources.*

What if we only have 50 minutes?
- ▶ Take 15 minutes to do the *Beginning* section all together.
  - You may have time for only two of the three questions.
- ▶ Then split up into sub-groups of four each for the Bible study.
- ▶ Reserve the last five minutes for the sub-groups to come back together.
  - Then the leader can give a concluding summary.
  - Or the sub-groups can report on what they learned.

Where should we meet?
- ▶ In a home is best (since everybody is comfortable in a home).
- ▶ But anywhere will work as long as:
  - You can all sit around in a circle facing each other.

What do we do when we meet?
- ▶ Each small group session has three parts to it:
  - *Beginning:* in which you share personal stories
  - *Understanding the Text:* in which you dig into what the text means
  - *Applying the Text:* in which you let the text speak to you personally

What if we don't have enough time to cover all this?
- ▶ Don't try to discuss all the questions (the leader will select the key ones).
- ▶ Break up into sub-groups of four to allow more interaction time for each person.
- ▶ Best of all: expand the time of each session from 60 to 90 minutes.

Will we have enough questions for a 90-minute discussion?
- ▶ Generally you will, but if you don't, you can use the *Optional Questions* and *Exercises.*
- ▶ The *Optional Questions* can also be assigned for homework.
- ▶ The advantage of more time is that the open-ended questions can be discussed more thoroughly.

Is homework necessary?
- ▶ No, the group can meet together with no prior preparation.
- ▶ Homework does extend and expand the personal impact of the Bible study.

What is the purpose of the *Reflection Questions?*
▶ To assist individuals in applying the material in a personal way
▶ To facilitate recollection of the past and how it affects present spiritual growth

Can *Journal* entries be shared with the group?
▶ Yes, as long as everyone knows ahead of time that this will be done.
▶ In this way, not only will people work on their *Journal* reflections during the week, but they can select what to share.

What role can sharing *Journal* entries play in the small group process?
▶ This is a great way to tell your story to others.
▶ This deepens the impact of each lesson by following up the next week with practical applications of the ideas that come from group members.
▶ This brings the group into our decisions to change, and it makes us accountable to the group in a healthy way.

Who leads the group?
▶ Anyone can lead the group. Prior to the meeting, he or she must be willing to spend an hour or so to go over all the materials and to read the *Small Group Leader's Notes* for that session.
▶ The role of the leader is to facilitate conversation, not to teach or counsel.
▶ Shared leadership is often good. In this way, no individual can begin to dominate the group.
▶ However, certain people seem to be better at leading discussions than others, and they should probably be allowed to exercise this gift.
▶ Even in this case, it is a good idea to give new leaders experience in running the group so they can develop their skills.

GROUP COVENANT: every member should consider his or her responsibilities to the group and agree.

▶ **Attendance:** to be at the session each week, unless a genuine emergency arises
▶ **Participation:** to enter enthusiastically into the group discussion and sharing
▶ **Confidentiality:** not to share with anyone outside the group the stories of those in the group
▶ **Honesty:** to be forthright and truthful in what is said; if you do not feel you can share something, say "I pass" for that question
▶ **Openness:** to be candid with the others in appropriate ways
▶ **Respect:** not to judge others, give advice, or criticize
▶ **Care:** to be open to the needs of each other in appropriate ways

Chapter One
Loving Others

Overview

We are commanded to love God; we are also commanded to love people. These two commandments come as no great surprise to us, nor do we find them odious. We all agree that love is a good thing and that we should love not only God but other people. Nobody goes around saying that what this world needs now is more hatred.

But the problem is that loving others is not always easy. People rub against us in abrasive ways; they do dumb and inconsiderate things; they are selfish; and they don't always appreciate us! So the art of loving others—all others and not just those we really like—is an art to be learned. This is the theme of the next seven lessons. As with learning to love God and learning to love ourselves, learning to love others is a lifelong task.

We will explore the question of loving others through a Bible study in which we examine Paul's great hymn to love in 1 Corinthians 13; through an essay on the art of loving drawn from Eric Fromm's famous book by that title; and by means of reflection on the relational world we inhabit.

The hope is that in the small group experience and through your own study, you will grow in your understanding of what it means to love others properly.

Beginning (20 minutes)

"Someone Special"

We all have special people in our lives. Often the loving relationships we had as children continue to nurture us when we are adults.

1. Who did you especially love when you were a child (other than your mom and dad)? Tell the group about that person.
   - ❏ an aunt or uncle
   - ❏ a grandparent
   - ❏ a sibling
   - ❏ a pet
   - ❏ a neighbor
   - ❏ a teacher
   - ❏ a friend of the family
   - ❏ a chum

2. How did you express your love for that person? Give a concrete example if you can.

3. From your experience, what one trait from the list below best characterizes a loving person? Why?
   - ❏ patience
   - ❏ kindness
   - ❏ rejoices in truth
   - ❏ protectiveness
   - ❏ trust
   - ❏ hope
   - ❏ perseverance
   - ❏ lack of envy
   - ❏ not boastful
   - ❏ not conceited
   - ❏ never rude
   - ❏ unselfish
   - ❏ not easily angered
   - ❏ doesn't keep track of wrongs
   - ❏ doesn't delight in the sins of others

The Text

13 If I speak in the **tongues of men and of angels**, but have not **love**, I am only a **resounding gong or a clanging cymbal**. [2] If I have the **gift of prophecy** and can fathom all mysteries and all knowledge, and if I have a **faith** that can move mountains, but have not love, I am nothing. [3] If I **give all** I possess to the poor and surrender my **body to the flames**, but have not love, I gain nothing.

[4] Love is **patient**, love is **kind**. It **does not envy**, it **does not boast**, it is **not proud**. [5]It is **not rude**, it is **not self-seeking**, it is **not easily angered**, it keeps **no record of wrongs**. [6]Love does not delight in evil but rejoices with the truth. [7]It always **protects**, always **trusts**, always **hopes**, always **perseveres**.

[8] Love never fails. But where there are prophecies, they will **cease**; where there are tongues, they will be **stilled**; where there is knowledge, it will **pass away**. [9]For we know in part and we prophesy in part, [10] but when perfection comes, the imperfect disappears. [11]When I was a child, I talked like a child, I thought like a child, I reasoned like a child. When I became a man, I put childish ways behind me. [12]Now we see but a poor reflection as in a **mirror**; then we shall see face to face. Now I know in part; then I shall know fully, even as I am fully known.

[13]And now these three remain: faith, hope and love. But **the greatest** of these is love.

1 Corinthians 13
New International Version

Understanding the Text (20 minutes)

1 Corinthians 13 is one of the most memorable passages in the New Testament. It is a hymn in honor of love, and as such, gives us sound advice on how to love others.

1. Scan the three paragraphs and come up with a short title that describes the main thought in each:
   ◆ Paragraph One (verses 1–3)_____
   ◆ Paragraph Two (verses 4–7)_____
   ◆ Paragraph Three (verses 8–13)_____

2. Examine Paragraph One by answering the following questions:
   ▶ What are the four spiritual gifts Paul identifies here?
   ▶ Describe the nature of each of these gifts.
   ▶ What is Paul's conclusion about these gifts?
   ▶ How does love purify each of these gifts?

3. Examine Paragraph Two by answering the following questions:
   ▶ What are the characteristics of love (both positive and negative)?
   ▶ What is the nature of each of these characteristics?

4. Examine Paragraph Three by answering the following questions:
   ▶ In what way does love differ from the other spiritual gifts?
   ▶ What does Paul imply by contrasting imperfection and perfection?
   ▶ Why, do you suppose, is love greater than faith and hope?

Optional Exercise

Take five minutes and write a letter to a friend (perhaps the person you mentioned in the *Beginning* exercise) describing what love is, according to Paul. Get into sub-groups of four and read your letters to one another.

Applying the Text (20 minutes)

1. Explore the significance of Paragraph One:
   ▶ How do these insights help to explain how a person can be very religious and yet difficult to get along with?
   ▶ Each of the gifts mentioned are of value to other people, but not necessarily to the person possessing them. Why not? What is the function of spiritual gifts?
   ▶ What is the source of personal greatness, according to Paul?

2. Explore the significance of Paragraph Two:
   ▶ Rate yourself (from 1 to 10) in terms of how well you do in living out each of the characteristics of love (listed in the *Beginning* exercise): 1 = "I have mastered this trait"; 5 = "I understand this as well as most people"; 10 = "I still have to learn this trait."
   ▶ Which characteristic is the easiest for you to live out?
   ▶ Which of love's characteristics do you find the most difficult? Explain.
   ▶ Explain what Paul means when he says love:
      • protects   • trusts
      • hopes   • perseveres

3. To become the kind of person Paul describes in 1 Corinthians 13 is not an easy task. We can know what we should be and still fall short.
   ▶ Which of the following barriers prevent us from being fully loving persons?
      ❏ Unconsciousness: not seeing clearly how we actually relate to others
      ❏ Defensiveness: not being able to trust others
      ❏ Inadequate role models: not really knowing how to relate to others
      ❏ Stubbornness: not wanting to change relational patterns
      ❏ Pride: not wanting to be in relationships of mutuality
      ❏ Hiddenness: not wanting to be open with others
      ❏ Anger: not really liking others very much
      ❏ Pain: not wanting to admit our deep needs
      ❏ Need: not feeling loved ourselves
   ▶ Which issue best describes what you struggle with in becoming a loving person?

Optional Question

If love prevailed fully, what difference would it make in the:
   ▶ church?   ▶ home?
   ▶ nation?   ▶ business?
   ▶ television?

Bible Study Notes

Setting: This passage follows a lengthy discussion of the spiritual gifts. Apparently the Corinthian Christians were enamored of gifts like speaking in tongues and prophecy. Paul wants them to pursue a more excellent way (1 Corinthians 12:31)—the way of love. 1 Corinthians 13 is one of the most famous (and most powerful) passages written by this apostle. Paul first points out the primacy of love in contrast to other religious activities (verses 1–3). Then he describes the anatomy of love (verses 4–7). The passage ends with Paul pointing to the enduring quality of love, again in contrast to other religious activities (verses 8–13).

tongues of men and of angels: Even if he were a great linguist who spoke many languages; and if he knew the language of heaven, this gift would be mere noise without love.

love: The Greek word is *agape* and refers to the kind of love that gives without expectation of return. It is love that is not based on how one feels about the other person; instead, it is love based on the need of the other.

resounding gong or a clanging cymbal: Pagans used gongs and cymbals in their ceremonies.

gift of prophecy: The Spirit-given ability to speak a word of exhortation or instruction.

faith: The Spirit-given conviction that God's mighty power will accomplish a great task.

give all: The one who gives without love will realize no particular benefit on the Day of Judgment.

body to the flames: Even martyrdom—the ultimate sacrifice—loses its meaning if love is absent.

patient: Being slow to get angry at others—despite provocation.

kind: Doing good—even to those who provoke us.

does not envy: Not coveting or begrudging what others have.

does not boast: Self-effacing; not bragging.

not proud: Not viewing others as inferior; not looking down on others.

not rude: Not behaving disgracefully; not shaming others.

not self-seeking: Not insisting on our rights; giving up our due for the sake of others.

not easily angered: Not easily provoked; not touchy.

no record of wrongs: Someone who forgives and forgets.

protects: The New English Bible translates this: "there is nothing love cannot face."

trusts/hopes: Love never loses faith. Thus it endures.

perseveres: Love is tenacious, buoyed up by its confidence in the future (Fee).

cease/stilled/pass away: In the heavenly kingdom, there will be no need for prophecy (since it will have been fulfilled), tongues (since direct communication with God will be possible), or knowledge (since all will have been revealed).

mirror: The bronze mirrors of that day gave back only a flawed image.

the greatest: Love is the greatest, since God is love.

Comment

The Art of Loving   *by Erich Fromm*

Is love an art? Then it requires knowledge and effort. Or is love a pleasant sensation, which to experience is a matter of chance, something one "falls into" if one is lucky? This little book is based on the former premise, while undoubtedly the majority of people today believe in the latter.

Not that people think that love is not important. They are starved for it; they watch endless numbers of films about happy and unhappy love stories, they listen to hundreds of trashy songs about love—yet hardly anyone thinks that there is anything that needs to be learned about love.

This peculiar attitude is based on several premises which either singly or combined tend to uphold it. Most people see the problem of love primarily as that of being loved, rather than that of loving, of one's capacity to love. Hence the problem to them is how to be loved, how to be lovable. In pursuit of this aim they follow several paths. One, which is especially used by men, is to be successful, to be as powerful and rich as the social margin of one's position permits. Another, used especially by women, is to make oneself attractive, by cultivating one's body, dress, etc. Other ways of making oneself attractive, used both by men and women, are to develop pleasant manners, interesting conversation, to be helpful, modest, inoffensive. Many of the ways to make oneself lovable are the same as those used to make oneself successful, "to win friends and influence people." As a matter of fact, what most people in our culture mean by being lovable is essentially a mixture between being popular and having sex appeal.

A second premise behind the attitude that there is nothing to be learned about love is the assumption that the problem of love is the problem of an object, not the problem of a faculty. People think that to love is simple, but that to find the right object to love—or to be loved by—is difficult. This attitude has several reasons rooted in the development of modern society. One reason is the great change which occurred in the twentieth century with respect to the choice of a "love object." In the Victorian age, as in many traditional cultures, love was mostly not a spontaneous, personal experience which then might lead to marriage. On the contrary, marriage was contracted by convention—either by the respective families, or by a marriage broker, or without the help of such intermediaries; it was concluded on the basis of social considerations, and love was supposed to develop once the marriage had been concluded. In the last few generations the concept of romantic love has become almost universal in the Western world. In the United States, while considerations of a conventional nature are not entirely absent, to a vast extent people are in search of "romantic love" of the personal experience of love which then should lead to marriage. This new concept of freedom in love must have greatly enhanced the importance of the object as against the importance of the function.[1]

The Art of Bible Study

The Process of Application

Application is what Bible study is all about: applying what the Bible says to our lives. The Bible is not a textbook on religion with facts to be memorized. Nor is it a history of an ancient people which we read to know about other cultures. The Bible is the Word of God: alive, powerful, true, and able to change lives. When we let what we understand about a passage actually change us, then we have allowed the Bible to be the Bible.

Thus we need to learn how to move from interpretation to application. This is not always an easy step. Quite apart from anything else, the process of application is loaded with subjectivity. When it comes to observation and interpretation, we operate in the realm of the objective. But application moves us into the realm of the subjective, and we must be very cautious. The danger is that we will go beyond the text into our own wishes, needs, and desires—making the text say what we would like it to say, not what it actually says. Or we will apply the text in a way that could never have been intended—because we are looking at things through twentieth-century eyes. So we need special caution when it comes to application. We must stick close to the text. We must listen carefully to its challenges—even when it demands change on our part and we do not especially like what it says.

The Bible can change us—moving us to become the kind of people God wants us to be. It changes our:

◆ Minds, so that we think differently about the way things are. Our aim in Bible study is to develop a biblical world view.
◆ Hearts, so that we feel with new passion the needs and suffering of the world around us. Our aim in Bible study is to develop a biblical passion.
◆ Actions, so that we live differently. Our aim in Bible study is to develop a biblical lifestyle.

> **Example:** Consider question 2 in the *Applying the Text* section. In what ways is this an application exercise? What kind of change is in view here: of the mind, heart, actions, or all three?

Extra Reading

◆ *Love Within Limits: A Realist's View of 1 Corinthians 13* by Lewis Smedes (Eerdmans). A brilliant study of 1 Corinthians 13, which helps to lift the soaring words of Paul from the pages of the Bible into our daily lives.
◆ *The Four Loves* by C.S. Lewis (Harcourt, Brace, Jovanovich). Another of Lewis' lucid and scintillating studies, this time focusing on the anatomy of love.
◆ *Mere Christianity* by C. S. Lewis (Macmillan). See especially Book III, Chapters 6, 7, and 9.
◆ *The Art of Loving* by Erich Fromm (Harper & Row).
◆ *Testaments of Love: A Study of Love in the Bible* by Leon Morris (Eerdmans).
◆ *Love Has its Reasons: An Inquiry into New Testament Love* by Earl Palmer (Word).

- *Agape: An Ethical Analysis* by Gene Outka (Yale University Press). A scholarly analysis of *agape* love which traces the literature on the topic.
- *Agape and Eros,* by Anders Nygren (S.P.C.K.). A classic theological study of the subject of love.
- *Caring & Commitment: Learning to Live the Love We Promise* by Lewis Smedes (Harper & Row). This is a book about making and keeping commitments in relationships. Promise-keeping is the key to deep relationships, and Smedes explores the world of commitment with great insight.
- *The Love Command in the New Testament* by Victor Furnish (Abingdon).

Reflection Questions

To become a fully loving person is a lifelong task. We all fall short of this high calling and always will this side of heaven. Still, we are commanded to love others and so we struggle to do so. The clearer we are about how well and how badly we do when it comes to love the better able we are to grow in the art of love.

1. Read carefully the essay by Erich Fromm on "The Art of Loving." Where do you see yourself in what he says? What new insights do you have into your attitudes and behaviors?
   ▶ In what ways is "love an art"?
   ▶ In what ways do you try to make yourself lovable? What is appropriate? Inappropriate?
   ▶ Are you seeking to find an object to love, or to develop the facility to love?

2. Continue reflecting on the characteristics of love. How well do you do with each aspect of loving others? How can you grow in your ability to love others?

3. Who are the people in your life? Draw a series of concentric circles that express the nature of your relationships. For example, you might put God in the central circle. On the next circle would be your spouse; the next circle your children; the next circle your childhood family and relatives; etc. Then, beginning with those closest to you, reflect on the nature of each of your relationships. Use Paul's list of characteristics of love as the grid to assess how well or how poorly you are doing. Reflect on what needs to change in each relationship.

4. Think about how well you relate to strangers—the many anonymous people you meet during a week (e.g., gas station attendants, clerks at stores, people on the bus, other drivers on the road, etc.). In what ways do you act in a loving fashion to those who are anonymous? Are your responses to them (either positive or negative) different from your responses to people who are close to you?

---

[1] *The Art of Loving* by Erich Fromm (New York: Harper & Row, 1962), pages 1–3.

Journal

Chapter Two
Loving Our Families

Lucy in the *Peanuts* comic strip once commented: "I love the whole human race. It's just people I don't like." In her own, inimitable way, she was expressing a profound truth. It is one thing to affirm that, as Christians, we love others. It is another thing to love specific people.

The Bible is quite clear about where this loving of others needs to begin: in our own families. One of the Ten Commandments speaks about honoring your father and mother. Paul writes about family relationships. The family is the crucible in which we learn to love others.

We will explore the question of loving our families through a Bible study in which we examine what Paul has to say about relationships within the family (Ephesians 5:21–6:4); through an essay on the revolutionary new perspective on marriage which Paul describes in Ephesians; and by means of reflection on our families, both our childhood family and our present family.

The hope is that in the small group experience and through your own study, you will grow in your understanding of what it means to love those in your family.

Beginning (20 minutes)

Family

We don't have much choice when it comes to families. But this is good. In this way, we learn to love all kinds of different people.

1. Describe the family you grew up in—with all the siblings, aunts and uncles, grandparents, etc. who were part of your childhood experience.

2. What was the best thing about your family?
   - ❏ laughing together
   - ❏ our family meals
   - ❏ competing with one another
   - ❏ celebrating holidays
   - ❏ family vacations
   - ❏ watching TV together
   - ❏ talking
   - ❏ doing things together
   - ❏ debating
   - ❏ playing together
   - ❏ other: _____

3. What family traditions have you carried over into your current (or future) family?

The Text

²¹**Submit to one another** out of **reverence for Christ**.

²²**Wives, submit to your husbands** as to the Lord. ²³For the husband is the **head** of the wife as Christ is the head of the church, his body, of which he is the Savior. ²⁴Now as the church submits to Christ, so also wives should submit to their husbands in everything.

²⁵Husbands, **love your wives**, just **as Christ loved the church** and gave himself up for her ²⁶to make her holy, cleansing her by the washing with water through the word, ²⁷and to present her to himself as a radiant church, without stain or wrinkle or any other blemish, but holy and blameless. ²⁸In this same way, husbands ought to love their wives **as their own bodies**. He who loves his wife **loves himself.** ²⁹After all, no one ever hated his own body, but he feeds and cares for it, just as Christ does the church—³⁰for we are members of his body. ³¹"For this reason a man will leave his father and mother and be united to his wife, and the two will become **one flesh**." ³²This is a profound mystery—but I am talking about Christ and the church. ³³However, each one of you also must love his wife as he loves himself, and the wife must **respect** her husband.

6 **Children, obey your parents** in the Lord, for this is right. ²**"Honor your father and mother"**—which is the first commandment with a promise—³"that it may go well with you and that you may enjoy long life on the earth."

⁴**Fathers, do not exasperate** your children; instead, bring them up in the **training** and **instruction** of the Lord.

Ephesians 5:21–6:4
New International Version

Understanding the Text (20 minutes)

Family relationships are very important in the Bible. They are mentioned in various places by different writers (i.e., Exodus 20:12; Colossians 3:18–21; 1 Peter 3:1–7). The church is described by the metaphor of a family (Ephesians 2:19; 1 John 5:1–2). Failure to maintain the family disqualifies a person from certain church offices (e.g., 1 Timothy 3:4–5). In this passage, Paul gives some guidelines for harmonious family relationships.

1. In relationships:
   - ▶ What is the duty of everyone (5:21)?
   - ▶ What is the obligation of wives to husbands (5:22–24)?
   - ▶ What is the obligation of husbands to wives (5:25–33)?
   - ▶ How should children relate to parents (6:1–3)?
   - ▶ How should fathers relate to children (6:4)?

2. Examine the role of the wife:
   - ▶ What is the basis for the wife's response to her husband?
   - ▶ What does the analogy of Christ and the church teach about the relationship of a wife to her husband?
   - ▶ What is the parallel word to "submit" in verse 33? How does this word help us understand what Paul means by "submit"?

3. Examine the role of the husband:
   ▶ What is the basis for the husband's response to his wife?
   ▶ What did Christ do for the church?
   ▶ What does this analogy teach husbands?
   ▶ What does the concept of loving oneself teach the husband about relating to his wife?
   ▶ What is the mystery of marriage? The mystery of the church?

4. Examine the relationship between parents and children:
   ▶ Why should children obey their parents?
   ▶ What is the role of fathers?

Applying the Text (20 minutes)

1. Explore the relationship of wives to husbands:
   ▶ What is the difference between submission and obedience?
   ▶ How would a first-century Roman wife have heard the call to submit to her husband? Why are some contemporary women rightly wary of the concept of submission?
   ▶ What are the ways in which a wife submits to (respects) her husband?

2. Explore the relationship of husbands to wives:
   ▶ Why do you suppose Paul directs three times as many words to husbands as to wives?
   ▶ What are some of the ways in which husbands should love their wives?

3. Explore the relationship between parents and children:
   ▶ Why do you suppose Paul addresses only fathers and not mothers?
   ▶ What does it mean not to exasperate your children?
   ▶ What does it mean to instruct your children in the Lord?

4. Explore the concept of mutual submission:
   ▶ How does the idea of mutual submission improve relationships?
   ▶ What is the problem of one-way submission?
   ▶ How easy/difficult is it for you to put mutual submission into practice?
   ▶ In what relationships is mutual submission inappropriate?

5. What are the dangers of:
   ▶ Women submitting to all men (and not just husbands)?
   ▶ Men seeking obedience from wives?
   ▶ Children refusing to obey parents?
   ▶ Parents dominating children?
   ▶ Relationships based on strict lines of authority rather than mutual love and submission?

Optional Discussion

Discuss the "typical American family" in light of what Paul has written:
   ▶ How do husbands and wives go about making decisions? How do parents and children make decisions? What does Paul have to say to these cultural patterns?
   ▶ What does Paul have to say to the feminist? The non-feminist?
   ▶ What does Paul have to say to the dominating male? To the weak male?

Bible Study Notes

Setting: In the first half of the letter to the Ephesians (chapters 1–3), Paul describes how Jesus has created a new community (the church) by bringing together traditional enemies (Jew and Gentile). In the second half of the letter (chapters 4–6), he discusses how to make this new reality work in everyday life. This section discusses family relationships.

Submit to one another: This is the principle that controls each of the relationships which Paul discusses. Mutual submission was a striking new concept in the first century, when men owned wives, children, and slaves in the same way they would own property. It is this conciliatory (rather than domineering, demanding) attitude that makes relationships work. Mutual submission is made possible by "filling of the Spirit" (5:18).

reverence for Christ: The rationale for this new way of relationships. Christ is the head of the church.

Wives: That Paul addresses women directly as individuals who can act on their own would have been striking to the first-century reader (who would have expected wives to have been addressed through their husbands). In Christ, women have found a whole new identity.

submit: The wife is to yield (adapt to; give way to) to her husband. "Submission is something quite different from obedience. It is a voluntary self-giving to a lover whose responsibility is defined in terms of constructive care; it is love's response to love" (Stott).

to your husbands: This yielding is not "all women to all men" (as was customary in the first century), but only a wife to her husband.

head: The meaning of this term (probably) is "source" (as in "the head of the river") and carries with it the idea of honor, rather than "authority" (as in "ruler") which carries with it the idea of domination. The idea here is that woman has her origin in man (according to Genesis 2:18–23) in the same way that the Church has its origin in Christ. Had Paul wanted to convey the idea that men rule over women (as Christ rules over the Church), he would have used a different Greek word.

love your wives: For his part in mutual submission, the husband is called to devote himself to the good of his wife.

as Christ loved the church: Christ loved the Church by dying for her! Thus what a wife is asked to "submit to" is sacrificial love, not domineering authority.

as their own bodies: Husbands and wives have become one flesh.

loves himself: This assertion is based on the Great Commandment and its call to love others (in this case the wife) as one loves oneself.

one flesh: Sex within marriage is an outer expression of a deeper, inner bonding of spirit.

respect: Paul summarizes what he said about the relationship between husband and wife. The submission of which he speaks is not a cowing obedience, but a mutual respect of two people.

Children: Again, it is amazing that Paul addresses children directly and not through their parents. Furthermore, Paul does not just command children. He gives four reasons for what he says. Thus he treats children with respect, which was unusual in the first century.

obey your parents: The children's side of mutual submission consists of obedience ("be subject to," "follow," "listen to"). This is a stronger word than what he uses to describe the relationship between men and women. Still, it does not give unlimited power to parents.

"Honor your father and mother": This is the fifth commandment. To honor one's parents means more than just obeying them. It is an attitude of love, respect, and consideration.

Fathers: But parents have their obligations to children as well. In this case, Paul singles out fathers (who in the first century could be demanding autocrats—they "owned" their children, even having the right to put them to death).

do not exasperate: Parents need to be careful not to provoke hostile reactions on the part of their children. They do this if they are cruel or unreasonable, if they humiliate (rather than build up), and if they overindulge (rather than provide appropriate boundaries and expectations).

training: Also translated "discipline"; it has to do with the proper correction of children.

instruction: The emphasis here is on what is said to children.

Comment

Husbands and Wives: Reflections on Ephesians 5:21–33

by John R. W. Stott

There is little doubt what 'submission' meant in the ancient world in which disdain for women was almost universal. William Barclay sums it up: "The Jews had a low view of women. In the Jewish form of morning prayer there was a sentence in which a Jewish man every morning gave thanks that God had not made him "a Gentile, a slave or a woman".... In Jewish law a woman was not a person, but a thing. She had no legal rights whatsoever; she was absolutely in her husband's possession to do with as he willed.... The position was worse in the Greek world.... The whole Greek way of life made companionship between man and wife next to impossible. The Greek expected his wife to run his home, to care for his legitimate children, but he found his pleasure and his companionship elsewhere.... In Greece, home and family life were near to being extinct, and fidelity was completely non-existent... In Rome in Paul's day the matter was still worse... The degeneracy of Rome was tragic.... It is not too much to say that the whole atmosphere of the ancient world was adulterous.... The marriage bond was on the way to complete breakdown.... It is against this dark background that Paul's teaching shines with such a bright light. Yet we still have to ask precisely what is meant by 'headship' and 'submission'....

Taking the husband first, what Paul stresses is not his authority over his wife, but his love for her. Rather, his authority is defined in terms of loving responsibility. To our minds the word 'authority' suggests power, dominion and even oppression... Certainly, 'headship' implies a degree of leadership and initiative, as when Christ came to woo and to win his bride. But more specifically it implies sacrifice, self-giving for the sake of the beloved, as when Christ gave himself for his bride. If 'headship' means 'power' in any sense, then it is power to care not to crush, power to serve not to dominate, power to facilitate self-fulfillment, not to frustrate or destroy it. And in all this the standard of the husband's love is to be the cross of Christ, on which he surrendered himself even to death in his selfless love for his bride....

As for the wife's duty in the marriage relationship... the requirement of submission is a particular example of a general Christian duty, that is, the injunction 'wives submit' (verse 22) is preceded by the requirement that we are to 'submit to one another' (verse 21). If, therefore, it is the wife's duty as wife to submit to her husband, it is also the husband's duty as a member of God's new society to submit to his wife. Submissiveness is a universal Christian obligation. Throughout the Christian church, including every Christian home, submissiveness is to be mutual. For Jesus Christ himself is the paragon of humility. He emptied himself of his status and his rights, and humbled himself to serve. So in the new order which he had founded he calls all his followers to follow in his footsteps. 'Clothe yourselves, all of you, with humility towards one another.' Should not the wife even rejoice that she has the privilege of giving a particular demonstration in her attitude to her husband of the beauty of humility which is to characterize all members of God's new society?[1]

The Art of Bible Study

The Art of Application

To discover the application of a passage is a three-step process. Each step consists of a different question to answer.

▶ *Step One:* How did the passage apply to those who first read it or lived it out?

▶ *Step Two:* What are the parallels between the application in the original setting and the issues in the twentieth century?

▶ *Step Three:* How does the passage apply to the various spheres of our lives?

Step One: It is vital to begin the application process with the original situation. One of the common mistakes in Bible study is to leap too quickly to the contemporary situation without having first probed how the original readers applied the text to their lives. Step One forces us to reflect on the application in the first century (in the case of the New Testament). It forces us to stay with the text.

> ***For example:*** Consider the optional exercise in *Understanding the Text.* You are asked to think about what Paul's words meant to those who first heard them. In this way the radical nature of his concepts is revealed and so, too, is the first-century application of this text.

Step Two: But then we must begin to move to our own situation. We do this by looking for contemporary parallels to the original situation. Notice that we do not immediately jump to personal application. First we need to notice the general situation in both its original context and the twentieth century. In this way, we help guard against missing important applications by viewing the text only through the lens of our own situation.

> ***For example:*** In both questions 1 and 4 in *Applying the Text,* the question is raised about what submission means—in the first century and now in these days of the feminist movement.

Step Three: Once we have some clarity as to the parallels that exist to our own situation, we can then become more personal in our attempts to apply the text to ourselves. The key in this step is to be forthright and honest, admitting to areas that need change in our lives. If we pretend we are perfect Christians with perfect families, jobs, and churches, the text can never reach us.

> ***For example:*** In question 4 in *Applying the Text* the question is asked: How easy/difficult is it for you to put mutual submission into practice? This moves the discussion to the personal level.

Extra Reading

There are numerous books available that deal with the relationships within a family. What follows is a selection that discusses parenting, dealing with troubled children, single parenting, blended families, and the relationship between spouses.

◆ *The Encyclopedia of Christian Parenting* (Revell). An easy-to-use reference book written by psychologists, doctors, and other professionals.

◆ *You Can Have a Family Where Everybody Wins* by Earl Gaulke (Concordia). A Lutheran pastor gives good advice about how love works in a family.

- *Self Esteem: A Family Affair* by Jean Isley-Clarke (Harper & Row).
- *"But You Don't Understand": How to Know You're Doing the Right Thing With Your Kids* by Paul Borthwick (Nelson).
- *Preparing for Adolescence: From Sexual Anxiety to Self-Esteem* by James Dobson (Bantam).
- *All Grown Up and No Place to Go* and *The Hurried Child: Growing Up Too Soon Too Fast* by David Elkind (Addison-Wesley).
- *Parents and Teenagers* by Jay Kesler (Victor). Advice from over fifty Christian leaders about the process of parenting.
- *Relief for Hurting Parents* by Buddy Scott (Oliver Nelson).
- *Parents in Pain* by John White (InterVarsity). The story of how White (a Christian psychiatrist) and his family coping with a deeply disturbed child.
- *Parents Without Partners Sourcebook* by Stephen Atlas (Running Press). Hands-on advice from scores of single parents.
- *How to Win as a Stepfamily* by Emily and John Visher (Dembner Books).
- *As For Me and My House: Crafting Your Marriage to Last* by Walter Wangerin, Jr. (Nelson. An excellent discussion written from a Christian point of view.
- *The Mystery of Marriage: As Iron Sharpens Iron* by Mike Mason (Multnomah). An award-winning book by a Canadian Anglican lay minister.

Reflection Questions

Families are not always places of great joy; they can also be places of great anguish. Explore your family situation: both your childhood family and your current family.

1. *Family of Origin:* Reflect on the nature and quality of relationships in your childhood family:
   ▶ Who were the key people for you in your family when you were growing up? Who loved you? Who did not really love you?
   ▶ Now as an adult, what are your relationships like with the members of your childhood family?
      • What were the best things about your family when you were growing up?
      • How functional/dysfunctional was your family? What was your "family secret" (if any) that you kept to yourselves? How did this affect you?
   ▶ What impact did your family have on:
      • your self-image?
      • your concept of a family?
      • the needs in your life today?

2. *Present Family:* Reflect on the nature and quality of relationships in your present family (however that is shaped):
   ▶ Who are the key people in your family? With whom are you the closest? Most distant? Why?
   ▶ What works well and what needs improvement in your relationship with your spouse? Children? Ex-spouse?
   ▶ What are the best things about your family?
   ▶ How can you improve family life?

---

[1] *God's New Society: The Message of Ephesians* by John R. W. Stott (InterVarsity, 1979), pages 224–225, 231–233.

Journal

Chapter Three
Fellowship With Others

Overview

If the family is the first place where we learn to love one another, the church is the second place. There, in a community made up of other men, women, and children who are striving to follow Jesus, we learn the lessons of love that we carry with us out into less hospitable situations.

At its best, Christian fellowship—*koinonia*—is an awesome force that melts hearts and mends lives. This experience of community is what we all long for but seldom realize. In this session, we will examine the character of true fellowship so that each of us can be agents of fellowship.

We will explore the nature of fellowship through a Bible study in which we look at three texts that describe the three parts of fellowship: mutual love, burden-bearing, and the spirit of unity (John 15:12–17; Galatians 6:1–2; Ephesians 4:1–6); through an essay which considers why true fellowship doesn't happen all the time; and by means of reflection on our own experiences of fellowship.

The hope is that in the small group experience and through your own study, you will grow in your understanding of what fellowship is and how to achieve it.

Beginning (20 minutes)

Socializing

We are social creatures, all of us: parties, celebrations, holidays, vacations—we enjoy getting together with others. Still, we have preferences.

1. What kind of social occasion do you like best? Recount one such event.
   - ❏ weddings
   - ❏ small group Bible study
   - ❏ baptisms
   - ❏ neighborhood parties
   - ❏ family dinners
   - ❏ church socials
   - ❏ all of the above
   - ❏ What I like best is: _____
   - ❏ holiday dinners
   - ❏ coffee (or tea) with friends
   - ❏ barbecues on the beach
   - ❏ any party
   - ❏ Saturday night with friends
   - ❏ dinners with friends at a nice restaurant
   - ❏ none of the above

2. Which of these events above do you most hate to attend? Why?

3. In your experience, what are the elements of the ideal party?

The Text

¹²"This is my **commandment**, that you **love** one another as I have loved you. ¹³Greater love has no man than this, that a man **lay down his life** for his friends. ¹⁴You are my friends if you do what I command you. ¹⁵ No longer do I call you **servants**, for the servant does not know what his master is doing; but I have called you friends, for all that I have heard from my Father I have made known to you. ¹⁶ You did not choose me, but I chose you and appointed you that you should go and **bear fruit** and that your fruit should abide; so that whatever you ask the Father in my name, he may give it to you. ¹⁷ This I command you, to love one another."

John 15:12–17
Revised Standard Version

6 Brethren, if a man is **overtaken in any trespass**, you who are **spiritual** should restore him in a **spirit of gentleness**. Look to yourself, lest you too be tempted. ²**Bear one another's burdens** and so fulfill **the law of Christ**.

Galatians 6:1–2
Revised Standard Version

4 As a **prisoner for the Lord**, then, I **urge** you to live a life worthy of the calling you have received. ²Be **completely humble** and **gentle**; be **patient**, **bearing with one another** in love. ³ **Make every effort** to **keep the unity** of the Spirit through the bond of peace. ⁴ There is **one body and one Spirit**— just as you were called to one **hope** when you were called—⁵one **Lord**, one **faith**, one **baptism**; ⁶**one God** and Father of all, who is over all and through all and in all.

Ephesians 4:1–6
New International Version

Understanding the Text (20 minutes)

It has been said that true fellowship is characterized by three things: mutual love, burden-bearing, and a spirit of unity.¹ We will examine three short texts which deal with these three issues.

1. Examine the John 15 passage (and the concept of mutual love) by answering the following questions:
   ▶ What is Jesus' twice-repeated command?
   ▶ What is a "command"? Who has the right to give commands? What ought to be our response to an appropriate command?
   ▶ Upon what example are we to pattern our love for others?
   ▶ What is the ultimate demonstration of love for others?
   ▶ What is the difference between a servant and a friend?
   ▶ Why were the disciples chosen?
   ▶ What is the fruit they are to bear?

2. Examine the Galatians 6 passage (and the concept of burden-bearing) by answering the following questions:
   ▶ What is our responsibility to other Christians caught in sin?
   ▶ What should our attitude be to such a person?
   ▶ What lesson is there for us in this situation?
   ▶ What are we commanded to do? Why?

3. Examine the Ephesians 4 passage (and the concept of unity) by answering the following questions:

▶ What is the nature of the behavior that is "worthy of our calling"?

▶ What are the five virtues that promote unity? How does each bring about or sustain unity?

▶ What does it mean to bear with one another in love?

▶ What is the unity which we are to preserve?

▶ What do we have in common with other believers that serves as the basis for this unity?

Optional Question

What are some of your best memories of fellowship in your church? When did you experience this fellowship? Why did it happen, do you suppose? How can such fellowship become a regular part of your church life (if it is not already so)? In what ways have you experienced fellowship as a member of this small group?

Applying the Text (20 minutes)

1. Explore the significance of the John 15 passage by answering the following questions:

▶ According to John 15, what is the nature of mutual love?

▶ In what ways does this kind of love provide the foundation for fellowship?

▶ What would the "fellowship" be like in a church without mutual love?

▶ How can you express mutual love to those in your church?

2. Explore the significance of the Galatians 6 passage by answering the following questions:

▶ How are we to respond to each other's burdens?

▶ In our society, how do people usually react when other people have problems?

▶ What attitudes encourage you to share your problems with others? Discourage you from doing so?

▶ How do you carry each other's burdens within your church fellowship?

3. Explore the significance of the Ephesians 4 passage by answering the following questions:

▶ According to Ephesians 4, why should we maintain unity in the church?

▶ How do the attitudes mentioned here make unity a realistic possibility?

▶ Why is there often disunity in the church?

▶ What are some practical and specific ways that unity can be maintained in your church?

▶ How are unity and fellowship connected?

Optional Exercise

Imagine that you are part of a team starting up a church in a new housing development. How would you plan the church so that deep fellowship is central to its nature? What specifically would you do to ensure that mutual love, burden-bearing, and unity prevailed?

Bible Study Notes

John 15

Setting: This is a selection from a long conversation Jesus had with his disciples just before his death. He told them what lay ahead, and gave them their "marching orders."

commandment: An order issued by the one in charge. In the case of Jesus, what he commanded was always for the good of others. The command to love is a command that brings purpose and fulfillment to life.

love: *Agape* love; i.e., self-giving love.

lay down his life: The disciples are confused by all that has been happening and by what Jesus is now saying to them. The experience of being his disciples has not turned out the way they expected. Shortly, however, they will see how much he loves them when he voluntarily gives up his life for them (and for all the world).

servants: Those who do the bidding of their master. In the first century, this often meant unquestioning obedience without any awareness of the reasons for orders. But Jesus does not treat his disciples in this way. They are his friends and so he explains what lies ahead.

bear fruit: Jesus' disciples are to bring forth the "fruit of the Spirit": love, joy, peace, patience, etc. (see Galatians 5:22–23). They are to exhibit his character in this world.

Galatians 6

Setting: In this section (Galatians 5:26–6:5), Paul describes what is involved in walking by the Spirit (5:25). The evidence of walking by the Spirit is found in loving other people.

overtaken in any trespass: Paul gives a particular example of burden-bearing: dealing with a Christian who is found in sin.

spiritual: Paul addresses his remarks to the mature Christians in the community.

restore: The Greek word here is also used in reference to mending broken fishing nets, setting broken bones, or bringing together different factions.

spirit of gentleness: There is no "laying down the law," "feeling superior" or "getting tough." Love for the fallen person is the basic attitude which makes us gentle.

tempted: To be tempted is to face a choice: to give in to what we know is wrong or to resist it.

Bear one another's burdens: The emphasis here is on helping one another to deal with sin. The Greek word translated "burden" means a "weight" or "heavy load" which is too much for one person to bear alone.

the law of Christ: The teachings of Jesus. The law of Christ is to love one another.

Ephesians 4

Setting: In the second half of this letter, Paul urges Christians to maintain the spirit of unity between diverse peoples who have been brought together by the reconciling death of Jesus. This unity is given expression in the Church.

prisoner for the Lord: When Paul wrote this letter, he was under house arrest as a "prisoner of Rome." In fact, his true and willing bondage was to Jesus Christ.

urge: Paul exhorts his readers (with the full weight of his apostolic authority) to embrace an entirely new way of life.

completely humble: This is the first of five qualities of life that promote bonding between people. Within first-century Greek culture, humility was understood to be the attitude of slaves. Christianity considered humility as the absence of pride and self-assertion.

gentle: Strength under control; not, as it is sometimes understood, the meekness of the timid.

patient: A refusal to avenge wrong or to retaliate quickly when others offend.

bearing with one another: A tolerance of the faults and foibles of others.

Make every effort: Fellowship requires effort to make it happen, and zeal to guard and sustain it.

keep the unity: This is what each of the five virtues seeks to promote: the close bonding of those who are the children of God.

one: Paul identifies the various aspects of this new unity. People are bound together because in Christ they share so much in common. Paul repeats the word "one" seven times in three verses as he identifies the basis on which their unity is founded.

one body and one Spirit: It is the Holy Spirit who creates and sustains the Church.

hope/Lord/faith/baptism: Jesus is the object of their common faith and hope; the one in whose name they are baptized.

one God: They all share the same heavenly Father.

Comment

Loving Ain't So Easy

What went wrong? Why isn't there more of the fellowship in our churches that we read about in the New Testament? Why does it seem that we are better at fighting with each other than loving each other?

There are many reasons for our failure to live out the fellowship we long for:

◆ Our sinful natures must rank as the top candidate for blame. Nobody has got it all together, and we bring our sin with us into the church. No wonder relationships often fall apart. But this is no big surprise. The New Testament assumes there will be a breakdown in relationships. This is why there is so much good advice about mending relationships.

◆ The New Testament church didn't seem to get it right any better than we do. At first, it all worked wonderfully. We only have to read Acts to be amazed by the quality of life among the early Christians. But then we turn to Paul's letters and read about the squabbling in the Corinthian church. We hear him admonish the Church at Galatia. John tries to sort things out with the Ephesian church. Really, human beings have such a capacity to mess things up.

But despite all this, fellowship does happen. Maybe not all the time. Maybe not always in large congregational meetings. Maybe not always explosively. But there are always pockets of fellowship:

◆ In the Wednesday night Bible study for newly married couples, there is laughter, sharing, learning, and tears (sometimes) as these six new couples try to make sense out of marriage.

◆ At the Easter service, people were so overwhelmed by the amazing fact of the Resurrection that when the peace was passed, spontaneous hugging broke out all over the church. What began as a ritual was transformed into deep caring.

◆ When the pastor visited John and Alice after their baby died of sudden infant death syndrome, he gave them the love and practical support that saw them through their grief.

◆ In the adult Sunday school class, good relationships were being established. Many seekers came to the class to investigate Christianity, and stayed because they felt they "belonged." In the end, they gave their lives to Christ.

Of course, it's experiences like these that make us hungry for fellowship. Maybe we can't have it all the time, but we can have the real thing some of the time. Maybe we have to work at making this happen.

The Art of Bible Study

Step One: The Original Application

The Bible was written for a purpose. It reveals to us who God is, what his actions are, and what is expected of us in light of this reality. In other words, the Bible has vital information to guide and shape our lives. Application is the art of getting in touch with the Bible on the personal level. It is learning to hear clearly what God is saying to us, now.

But we, as contemporary readers, are not the only ones to whom God speaks. He has been speaking through the Bible to men and women down through the ages. And it is important to try to hear what God was saying to the original readers of the text. The various authors who penned the words of Scripture by the inspiration of the Holy Spirit did so with particular situations in mind. They sought to address certain questions (e.g., the questions the Corinthians wrote Paul about in 1 Corinthians 7:1), deal with specific problems (e.g., the false teaching in Colosse), give information (e.g., about Paul's well-being in Philippians 1:12), remind people of their history (e.g., the first five books of the Old Testament), and praise God for certain acts (e.g., the Psalms).

It is most important for us, as contemporary readers, to discover the original intention of the text. This is the original application of the text. Knowing this, we know the boundaries within which the text applies today. Thus we guard against any application not warranted by the text. In other words, we remain faithful to the text, rather than reading something into it.

So the first step in the application process is to investigate how a text applied to the original readers. This will involve some research on our part into the background and issues of these readers. However, we will have been doing this already in the interpretation process. So when we ask: "What was the application to the first readers?" we will already have some sense of how to answer that question.

In narrative accounts (such as the Gospels and other historical books), we can ask another question: "What was the application to each person in the story?" Again, this will give us the guidance we need to understand how the text applies to us.

Extra Reading

The issue of fellowship cannot be discussed apart from the Church, since it arises out of the very essence of the Church itself. The following books discuss the themes of fellowship, community, and the Church.

◆ *Paul's Idea of Community: The Early House Churches in their Historical Setting* by Robert Banks (Eerdmans). Dr. Banks describes the nature of community in early Christianity, looking especially at the community as a family and as a body. This is a thoughtful, highly provocative book.

◆ *Growth Groups: A Key to Christian Fellowship and Spiritual Maturity in the Church* by Michael Dibbert & Frank Wichern (Zondervan). A guide to establishing small groups as a means to promote and experience fellowship.

◆ *We Belong Together: The Meaning of Fellowship* by Bruce Milne (InterVarsity). An excellent study of fellowship.

- *Body Life* by Ray Stedman (Gospel Light). The experience of one church as it sought to create a warm, loving, caring community.
- *The Family and the Fellowship: New Testament Images of the Church* by Ralph Martin (Eerdmans). Dr. Martin analyzes with great skill and clarity key images for the church.
- *I Believe in the Church* by David Watson (Eerdmans). An excellent study of the nature of the church.
- *The Problem of Wine Skins: Church Structure in a Technological Age*); *The Community of the King*, and *A Kingdom Manifesto: Calling the Church to Live Under God's Reign* by Howard Snyder (InterVarsity). A fascinating series of books by a pastor-scholar who challenges us to rethink the nature of the church.
- *Community That Is Distinctively Christian* by Julie Gorman (Victor Books), 1993.
- *The People Called: The Growth of Community in the Bible* by Paul Hanson (Harper & Row).
- *Biblical Foundations for Small Group Ministry: An Integrational Approach* by Gareth Icenogle (InterVarsity).
- *Dangerous Memories: House Churches and our American Story* by Bernard J. Lee and Michael A. Cowan (Sheed & Ward).
- *Jesus and Community* by Gerhard Lohfink (Fortress Press).

Reflection Questions

We need each other. We need to be part of supportive, caring groups. One of the maladies of modern society is the loss of caring groups. People have moved out of the closeness of farm communities into the anonymity of cities. Neighborhoods have become mere bedrooms where we sleep, not communities where we are involved in the lives of our neighbors. Clubs are mostly a thing of the past. Families now cluster around televisions so an evening without conversation is the norm.

As individualism grows, so does our need for true fellowship. How are your needs for fellowship being met?

1. In your past:
   ▶ What groups were you a part of? What impact did these groups have on you?
   ▶ What were your best experiences of community? Your worst?

2. In your present:
   ▶ Who are the people (outside your family) with whom you have a close connection?
   ▶ What are your needs for fellowship? How can you begin to realize these?

3. In your Christian experience:
   ▶ What have been your best experiences of Christian fellowship? Your worst?
   ▶ How are your needs for Christian fellowship being met?

---

[1] *Baker's Dictionary of Theology*, (Grand Rapids: Baker), page 219.

Journal

Chapter Four
Getting Along with Others

Overview

Christian community is one of the great blessings in this life. Fellowship with others who seek to follow Jesus is a great encouragement and joy.

But it is also true that getting along with other Christians can be one of the great problems in life! Our fallen natures express themselves even in our church life, and sometimes we're more likely to fight with other Christians than embrace them.

The causes for these divisions are many; sometimes we differ over lifestyle issues. In particular, some people feel that if a person is truly Christian, he or she will follow a certain code of behavior. This code is often characterized by a series of taboos which must be avoided. But other Christians (who agree that certain behaviors are prohibited in Scripture) feel that most behaviors are a matter of preference, and that there is great freedom in how we live. Who is right? Those who are strict or those who are lenient? Those who are bound or those who are free? And how do we live with these differences?

Conflict over lifestyle is not a new issue in the church. As we will see in Romans 14, such tensions were a part of the first-century church.

We will explore the tension between rules and freedom in the Christian life through a Bible study in which we look at principles that help us to deal with differing views on lifestyle (Romans 14); through comments on diversity in lifestyle; and by means of reflection on conflicts we had over lifestyle issues.

The hope is that through the small group experience and through your own study, you will grow in your understanding of how to get along with people in the church who hold different convictions.

Beginning (20 minutes)

Taboo

"Don't do it!" Every child knows these words. This is what taboos are all about: prohibitions against certain behavior. All societies and groups have taboos. Some are good, some are bad; most are a matter of conscience.

1. What taboos did you have when you were a child?
   - ❐ Don't swear.
   - ❐ Don't play with girls (or boys).
   - ❐ Don't drink.
   - ❐ Don't eat sweets.
   - ❐ Don't _____.
   - ❐ Don't talk to strangers.
   - ❐ Don't stay out after dark.
   - ❐ Don't smoke.
   - ❐ Don't sass your mother.

2. Which taboos did you keep? Why?

3. Which taboos did you break? Why?

The Text

¹⁰ **Why do you pass judgment** on your brother? Or you, **why do you despise** your brother? For we shall all stand before the judgment seat of God; ¹¹for it is written,

> "As I live, says the Lord,
>   every knee shall bow to me,
>   and every tongue shall give praise
>   to God."

¹² So each of us shall give account of himself to God.

¹³Then let us no more pass judgment on one another, but rather decide never to put a **stumbling block** or hindrance in the way of a brother. ¹⁴I know and am persuaded in the Lord Jesus that **nothing is unclean in itself**; but it is unclean for any one who thinks it unclean. ¹⁵If your brother is being injured by what you eat, you are no longer walking in love. Do not let what you eat **cause the ruin** of one for whom Christ died. ¹⁶So do not let what is good to you be spoken of as evil. ¹⁷For the kingdom of God does not mean food and drink but **righteousness and peace and joy in the Holy Spirit**; ¹⁸he who thus serves Christ is acceptable to God and approved by men.

¹⁹Let us then pursue what makes for peace and for **mutual up-building**. ²⁰Do not, for the sake of food, destroy the work of God. Everything is indeed clean, but it is wrong for any one to make others fall by what he eats; ²¹ it is right not to eat meat or **drink wine** or do anything that **makes your brother stumble**.

²² The faith that you have, **keep between yourself and God**; happy is he who has no reason to judge himself for what he approves. ²³But he who has doubts is condemned, if he eats, because he does not act from faith; **for whatever does not proceed from faith is sin**.

Romans 14:10–23
Revised Standard Version

Understanding the Text (20 minutes)

One of the issues in Romans 14 is whether Christians could, with a clear conscience, eat foods that had probably been offered to idols. This is not a particular problem for most of us today. But the guidelines that Paul gives to solve this problem (and the problem of going against Old Testament food and Sabbath taboos) are still of great value when we confront people in the church who hold differing convictions about what constitutes a Christian lifestyle.

1. Examine paragraph one (verses 10–12):
    ▶ What are "weak" Christians not to do to those who hold different convictions?
    ▶ What are "strong" Christians not to do to those who hold different convictions?
    ▶ Why not?

2. Examine paragraph two (verses 13–18):
    ▶ What is the first principle that is articulated here (verse 14)?
    ▶ What is the second principle noted here (verse 15, see also verse 13)?
    ▶ Given these principles, what does this say about the kingdom of God (verse 17)?

3. Examine paragraphs three and four (verses 19–23):
  ▶ What is the goal for which we should strive?
  ▶ How does this goal relate to faith?

Optional Exercise

Paul summarizes his argument in verses 20–23. Put into your own words what he says here. Read your paraphrases to one another.

Applying the Text (20 minutes)

1. Which of the following "Christian taboos" have you encountered? Where and when? How did you feel about the taboo? Which of these activities (if any) do you avoid as a matter of conviction?
  ❏ no smoking or drinking
  ❏ no dancing
  ❏ no associating with people outside your church
  ❏ no version of the Bible accept the King James Version
  ❏ no movies
  ❏ no swimming in mixed-gender groups
  ❏ no reading the newspaper on Sunday
  ❏ no eating meat (or some other dietary regulation)

2. What do you think about the following "voluntary obligations" that some Christians adopt for themselves?
  ❏ giving up something for Lent
  ❏ giving money (beyond the tithe) for the sake of the poor
  ❏ living in places of great need as agents of the gospel
  ❏ offering to work on projects that benefit the needy

3. Explore the question of relating to Christians who hold different convictions:
  ▶ How do you react to a person who holds an opposite view to yours about an activity, and firmly believes he or she is right and you are dead wrong? If possible, give an actual example of this, and talk about how you dealt with it (properly or not).
  ▶ According to Romans 14, how can the two of you stay in fellowship?
  ▶ What is the difference between deferring to a new Christian (who is sorting out his or her faith) and being bound by an old "Pharisee" (with lots of taboos)?

Optional Exercise

Whether or not you may have a second helping of roast beef is not an issue covered in the Bible. Consider this issue using the principles in Romans 14 to guide you:
  ▶ Suppose you have a seriously overweight person at the table who is struggling to diet. How does the principle in verse 15 help: "Do not let what you eat cause the ruin of one for whom Christ died"?
  ▶ Now suppose that instead of an overweight person there is a committed vegetarian at the table (who feels that vegetarianism is the Christian way). How does the principle in verse 13 help: "Never...put a stumbling block or hindrance in the way of a [person]"?
  ▶ You take a second helping, and the vegetarian takes exception to what you have done. What do you say?

Bible Study Notes

Setting: In this passage Paul addresses an issue that threatened to split the Roman church. While it is not possible to identify the contending parties precisely, the root issue is clear. One group (the "strong") believed that all the old taboos about food and sacred days were abolished when Jesus came. The other group (the "weak") believed that Christians were still bound by these ceremonial laws. The question that the Church faced was how to maintain its unity in the face of strong feelings on both sides of the issue.

pass judgment/despise: There are two forms of judgment. The "strong" look down upon, laugh at, or fail to take seriously the scruples of the "weak." On the other hand, the "weak" condemn what appears to be a lack of conviction on the part of the "strong," and they become critical and haughty. Both of these attitudes are wrong; both break fellowship. God alone has the right to judge others. In any case, both the weak Christian and the strong Christian belong to God.

Why do you pass judgment: Addressed to the "weak" Christian.

why do you despise: Or "look down upon"; words addressed to the "strong" Christian.

stumbling block: Something that causes a person to fall into sin. For example, don't eat meat in front of a Christian whose scruples do not allow him to eat meat. This might cause him to ignore his conviction and try the meat, which would be sin for him (verses 14, 23). The very freedom of the "strong" can harm others.

nothing is unclean in itself: This is an amazing statement for a former Pharisee like Paul to make. His life had once been defined by the strict avoidance of all kinds of activities. Now that he is a Christian, he has come to see that these taboos are of no spiritual consequence. See also Acts 10:9–23 for the account of how Peter came to realize the same truth.

cause the ruin: By causing a person to go against his convictions.

righteousness and peace and joy in the Holy Spirit: The kingdom of God is not about such trivial matters as food taboos, but about right living—a new relationship with God (peace with God), and the joy the Holy Spirit brings.

mutual up-building: The aim of all Christians is to build up one another; i.e., to help each other grow in the Lord.

drink wine: The Old Testament does not forbid the drinking of wine, except for priests when they are on duty (Leviticus 10:9) and those who were Nazarites (Numbers 6:2–4). But in Rome, wine may have been associated with pagan rituals (and was thus suspect for some).

makes your brother stumble: The strong Christian's right to freedom (in matters of behavior) must be balanced with concern about the well-being of weaker Christians.

keep between yourself and God: Strong Christians are not asked to give up their convictions; they are advised not to flaunt them (when doing so might confuse or mislead others).

whatever does not proceed from faith is sin: To go against deeply-held convictions is, in fact, sin.

Comment

C. S. Lewis once commented that Christians are the only ones who can drink alcohol, since they understand moderation.

Augustine said: "Love God and do as you please."

The basis of our freedom as Christians is the fact that "nothing is unclean in itself" (verse 14). Therefore it is permissible to do anything (except those things expressly forbidden, such as murder and lying). However, we are not allowed complete freedom, because certain activities may be a "stumbling block" (verse 13) to others, or they may not result in "peace and mutual upbuilding" (verse 19) or "joy in the Holy Spirit" (verse 17). Likewise, we sometimes temper our actions because our liberty might harm our brother or sister in the faith (verse 15).

As Christians we are not bound by a long list of "do's" and "don'ts." We are free to choose how we act. In Paul's day, the pagan (and the Jew, to a certain extent) was bound. Such people had numerous regulations and restrictions which they followed in order to please their gods (or the God of Israel). Christ delivered us from all of this and made us free. We have been given guidelines (rather than strict rules) to live our lives by. Our aim is to apply these guidelines conscientiously and in a way that will promote mutual well-being.

On Matters of Indifference   *by William Barclay*

One man will genuinely see no harm in playing some outdoor game on the Sabbath; and he may be right; but another man's whole conscience is shocked at such a thing, and, if he were persuaded to take part in it, all the time he would have the lurking and haunting feeling that he was doing wrong.

Paul's advice is quite clear. It is a Christian duty to think of everything, not as it affects ourselves only, but also as it affects others. Now, note, that Paul is not saying that we must always allow our conduct to be dominated and dictated by the views, and even the prejudices, of others; there are matters which are essentially matters of principle, and in them a man must take his own way. But, there are a great many things which are neutral and indifferent; there are a great many things which are neither in themselves good or bad; there are a great many things which are really pleasures and pastimes, and habits and customs, which a man need not do unless he likes. They are not essential parts of life and conduct; they belong to what we might call the extras of life; and, it is Paul's conviction that in such things we have no right to give offence to the more scrupulous brother. We have no right to distress and outrage his conscience by doing them ourselves, or by persuading him to do them.[1]

The Art of Bible Study

Step Two: The Twentieth-Century Application

Once you understand the application of the text in the original situation, you can begin to look for parallels with our contemporary situation.

Sometimes this is very easy. Even though the original setting of the text is at least 2,000 years old, human problems remain surprisingly constant. As a result, there are times when we immediately understand the issue the first-century people were struggling with. For example, when we read about the different factions in the church at Corinth, we know the problem from our own experience. We have been in churches that have had factions, or we have read about such churches. Thus Paul's words are as appropriate and applicable to us as they were to the Corinthians.

But there are times when the problem does not apply to twentieth-century culture. For example, we do not immediately understand what the fuss was all about in the church at Rome over the question of eating meat. The problem was not that vegetarians objected to eating meat. Nor was it about hygiene (certain meats would make you sick), nor did it concern dietary restrictions for religious purposes. These are possibilities that we might impose on the situation from our twentieth-century perspective, but they are inaccurate. So we have to do research to understand the problem.

The problem was that most of the meat that was sold in Rome had been offered to idols. The Roman butchers were priests at pagan temples. The Roman Christians wondered if the meat was contaminated by this evil association. Clearly, this is a situation which is very different from our own (though Christians in some third-world countries would understand the problem immediately).

Once we have understood the original situation, we can look for similarities to our situation. Today, for example, some Christians have a taboo about drinking. (The Bible forbids drunkenness, not drinking.) Others have concerns about diet, planetary pollution, political activism, working on Sunday, or certain styles of worship. Each of these issues can cause divisions among Christians, especially when the issue becomes a matter of religious conviction. But once we have identified our parallel situation, we can apply Paul's principles for remaining together in fellowship.

Extra Reading

- ◆ *Flirting with the World: A Challenge to Loyalty* by John White (Harold Shaw). White feels that the Church sometimes fights over inessentials (like dress codes, playing cards, or going to the movies) while failing to notice the real issues (such as pride, materialism, and hypocrisy).
- ◆ *Taboo?* by C. S. Woods (Inter-Varsity). A booklet analyzing common attitudes toward worldliness and discussing its biblical meaning.
- ◆ *Right Living in a World Gone Wrong* by David Hubbard (InterVarsity).
- ◆ *Agenda for Biblical People* by Jim Wallis (Harper & Row).
- ◆ *The Race: Discipleship for the Long Run* by John White (InterVarsity). White writes with great clarity about issues of Christian living.

- *Consistent Christianity* by Michael Griffiths (InterVarsity).
- *Finding Spiritual Direction: The Challenge & Joys of Christian Growth* by Douglas Webster (InterVarsity). Using the letter of James, Webster challenges us to live a Spirit-filled life in the midst of the complexity and hectic nature of ordinary life.
- *Coloring Outside the Lines: Discipleship for the "Undiscipled"* by John F. Westfall (HarperSanFrancisco). An unusual but very refreshing look at Christian discipleship written by a self-described "night person" (who contends that most discipleship books are written by "morning people"). This is his attempt to rectify the problem by producing a book for people who don't fit the mold.
- *The Pursuit of Holiness* and *The Practice of Godliness* by Jerry Bridges (NavPress).
- *Conscience* by O. Hallesby (Augsburg). A classic discussion of the role of the conscience in the life of the Christian.
- *Your Conscience as Your Guide* by Peter Toon (Morehouse-Barlow). A useful update of the Hallesby book. Toon looks at the significance of conscience (in the Bible and Christian thought) as a guide to decision-making.
- *Guilt: Curse or Blessing* by Arthur Becker (Augsburg).
- *No Condemnation: Rethinking Guilt Motivation in Counseling, Preaching, and Parenting* by S. Bruce Narramore (Zondervan).

Reflection Questions

1. Make a list of people you have encountered who hold views opposite to yours—people with whom you have had some conflict. What was the nature of the conflict? Did they come across as judgmental to you? Did you scorn them for their outmoded views? Did you judge them for their "sub-Christian" views? Reflect on the nature of your differences in light of Romans 14. In what ways was your attitude toward them appropriate? Less than perfect?

2. How well do you relate to the "weaker" brother or sister? Are you comfortable with restraining yourself in certain situations? What activities should you reconsider as permissible, but not "the best"?

3. How well do you relate to the "stronger" brother or sister. How do you respond when they do something you think is anti-Christian? What activities are more a matter of law than of necessity to you?

4. How do you determine your behavior when it comes to matters which aren't dealt with in Scripture? Do you function with a "do whatever I can do" mentality? Or do you find it easier to abide by a lot of personal "rules" that circumscribe what you do? Or do you "go with the crowd," and let the group decide what is and isn't permissible? Reflect on where you need to loosen up (and where you need to reign in) your behavior.

---

[1] *The Letter to the Romans (The Daily Study Bible)*, translated and interpreted by William Barclay (Philadelphia: The Westminster Press, 1957), pages 206–207.

Journal

Chapter Five
Opposition From Others

Overview

It is not only within our Christian fellowship that we encounter people who differ with us and let us know they do. In fact, the strongest opposition to our Christian convictions generally comes from outside the church.

The opposition may be mild: we get teased about being "so religious." Or we get a chilly reception from some family members who find our Christian beliefs "a bit much." But the opposition may be considerable. We find ourselves passed over for promotion (or fired) because of our faith. Or we are ignored, sidelined, avoided, or laughed at because of how we live our lives. Or a group of people may systematically make life miserable for us because we are "one of those Christians."

The question remains: How do we deal with opposition which arises because of our Christian faith? This is not a new question. It was a burning issue in the first century, when being a Christian might get you killed (and almost certainly would get you persecuted). Peter, who addresses this question, has some wise words for us.

We will explore the issue of opposition through a Bible study in which we examine a passage written by Peter during a time when Christians were being persecuted for their faith (1 Peter 3:13–18); through an essay on the need to understand the reasons for our faith; and by means of reflection on our own experiences of being rejected or harassed because of our faith.

The hope is that through the small group experience and through your own study, you will grow in your understanding of how to handle opposition to your faith.

Beginning *(20 minutes)*

Arguments

Kids argue all the time, and over the strangest issues.

1. When you were a kid, what did you argue about?
   - ❏ which was the best team (football, baseball, etc.)
   - ❏ who was the smartest (prettiest, etc.)
   - ❏ which school was best (town, state, etc.)
   - ❏ who was the best musician (song, group, etc.)
   - ❏ who was the greatest movie star, (the best movie, etc.)
   - ❏ who could run fastest (hit a ball farther, etc.)

2. How well did you do in an argument as a kid?

3. When there is conflict now, what do you tend to do?
   - ❏ shout
   - ❏ withdraw
   - ❏ argue
   - ❏ avoid
   - ❏ cry
   - ❏ back off
   - ❏ mediate
   - ❏ wait
   - ❏ dominate
   - ❏ give in
   - ❏ run

The Text

⁸**Finally, all of you, live in harmony** with one another; **be sympathetic, love as brothers, be compassionate** and **humble**. ⁹**Do not repay evil** with evil or insult with insult, but with **blessing**, because to this you were called so that you may inherit a blessing. ¹⁰**For,**

> "Whoever would love life
> and see good days
> must keep his tongue from evil
> and his lips from deceitful speech.
> ¹¹He must turn from evil and do good;
> he must seek peace and pursue it.
> ¹²For the eyes of the Lord are on the righteous
> and his ears are attentive to their prayer,
> but the face of the Lord is against those who do evil."

¹³ **Who is going to harm you if you are eager to do good?** ¹⁴**But** even if you should suffer for what is right, you are blessed. "**Do not fear what they fear**; do not be frightened." ¹⁵But in your hearts **set apart Christ as Lord**. Always **be prepared** to **give an answer** to everyone who asks you to give the **reason** for the hope that you have. But do this with **gentleness and respect**, ¹⁶keeping a clear conscience, so that those who speak maliciously against your good behavior in Christ **may be ashamed** of their **slander**. ¹⁷It is better, if it is God's will, to suffer for doing good than for doing evil. ¹⁸For Christ died for sins once for all, the righteous for the unrighteous, to bring you to God.

1 Peter 3:8–18a
New International Version

Understanding the Text (20 minutes)

Our aim as Christians is to live in harmony with all people, as far as it is in our ability to do so. Sometimes, however, there will be opposition. Peter describes what our response should be.

1. Examine Peter's call for harmony (verses 8–12):
   ▶ What is the goal Peter defines for the Christian community?
   ▶ What attitudes and actions will promote harmony? Define them.
   ▶ According to the quotation from Psalm 34 (verses 10–12), what are the reasons for keeping the commands in verses 8–10?

2. Examine Peter's assertions about persecution (verses 13–15a):
   ▶ What is Peter's first assertion about avoiding persecution (verse 13)?
   ▶ What is Peter's second, qualifying assertion (verse 14)?
   ▶ What is the promise to those who "suffer for what is right"?
   ▶ What should our attitude be when we suffer opposition?
   ▶ What inner resource makes this possible?

3. Examine Peter's call to a thoughtful Christianity (verses 15b–16):
   ▶ What form of opposition does Peter allude to in verse 15b?
   ▶ What is our responsibility to those who call us to account for our beliefs?
   ▶ What attitudes should characterize our conversation with those who challenge our beliefs? Why?

4. Examine Peter's summary of how Christians should respond to slander and persecution (verses 17–18):
   ▶ What basic principle does he give us to follow?
   ▶ How does he illustrate this principle in the life of Christ?

Optional Exercise

The following are questions which we are likely to be asked about our Christian faith. Pick one or two of these and discuss together what your response might be.
   ▶ How can you say that Jesus is the the only way to God?
   ▶ How can you say Jesus rose from the dead?
   ▶ How can you say that God is all-powerful and all-loving, when there is so much suffering in the world?
   ▶ How can you say that the Bible is true when it is filled with contradictions?

Applying the Text (20 minutes)

1. Peter asserts that the first step in avoiding persecution is to live in a way that promotes harmony.
   ▶ Describe how each of the attitudes he lists promotes harmony:
      ◆ a sympathetic attitude   ◆ brotherly love
      ◆ compassion   ◆ humility
      ◆ not repaying evil with evil, but with blessing
   ▶ Give an example of how one of these attitudes defused a bad situation for you.

2. Peter also asserts that it is possible to be persecuted for doing what is right.
   ▶ Why do you think people would persecute someone for doing the right thing?
   ▶ Have you ever been the target of this sort of harassment? What happened?
   ▶ Which individuals give you a hard time about your faith, and how can you relate to them in a better way?

3. Sometimes, however, we experience opposition because of our bad manners or poor behavior. Imagine what might take place in the following situations:
   ▶ At every family gathering, a young man fervently proclaims the gospel message until he is no longer invited over by his relatives.
   ▶ A clerk complains constantly about how unchristian her workmates are in speech, attitude, and behavior.

4. We can be opposed for what we believe—not just for what we do.
   ▶ Why might Christian beliefs be a source of contention?
   ▶ If you were asked to explain why you believed in Jesus, how thorough would your response be?
   ▶ What steps can the average Christian take to increase his or her understanding of the faith?

Optional Exercise

Explore the difference between suffering for righteousness' sake and suffering for being a "pain in the neck":
   ▶ What attitudes do we sometimes show to those who are not Christians?
   ▶ Why do we act this way?
   ▶ How can we become agents of peace and harmony?

Bible Study Notes

Setting: The Roman Emperor Pliny used "to inquire whether people were Christians, to give them the opportunity to sacrifice to the Emperor's genius; and, if they refused, to execute them for contumacy" (insubordination).[1]

Finally: This is the conclusion of a series of remarks by Peter on the question of how his readers can "live such a good life among the pagans that, though they accuse you of doing wrong, they may see your good deeds and glorify God on the day he visits us" (2:12). He urges that they give due respect: respect to rulers (2:13–17); respect to slave owners even though they mistreat them (2:18–20); and respect by a wife to her pagan husband (3:1–6). Here he concludes these remarks by urging respect of fellow believers (3:8) and of enemies (3:9).

all of you: In his previous remarks, Peter has addressed slaves (2:18–25), wives (3:1–6), and husbands (3:7). Now, in the matter of suffering for doing good he addresses the whole Christian community.

live in harmony: This is the intention: to live in harmony with everyone, both inside and outside the Christian community. He then goes on (in verses 8–9) to describe the attitudes and actions that promote harmony. This is the first of five attitudes that define the way Christians should treat each other.

be sympathetic: They should seek to identify with the feelings of others.

love as brothers: They should maintain the kind of love that knit them together as a fellowshipping community.

be compassionate: They should respond to each other's suffering with great sympathy.

humble: They should not be puffed up with pride, but should consider others to be better than themselves (Philippians 2:3).

Do not repay evil: Now Peter describes how they are to relate to those who persecute them. For one thing, they are not to retaliate.

blessing: Instead, they are to surprise their foes and respond with a blessing.

For: Peter quotes Psalm 34:12–16. It gives the reasons for obeying his commands in verses 8–10. The Psalm states that the Lord will rescue his suffering children who trust in him.

Who is going to harm you if you are eager to do good?: Seeking to live in a way that promotes harmony is the best way to ward off persecution.

But: Still, this will not guarantee that a Christian will not suffer.

Do not fear what they fear: A quotation from Isaiah 8:12. This phrase can be translated "do not fear their threats." One of the dangers the Christians face is fear itself.

set apart Christ as Lord: Instead of fear, Jesus should be in their hearts and minds. An inner commitment to Jesus gives a Christian the ability to stand up to slander and persecution.

be prepared: A call to know the reasons for our faith. This is part of loving God with our minds. If people are asked about their faith, they must be able to provide a coherent explanation of what they believe and why they have such hope (even when they are suffering).

give an answer: Christianity is not a set of "cunningly devised fables," but a faith with historic reasons to support it. Chief among these is the solid, historical evidence that Christ rose from the dead.

reason: Greeks especially valued an intelligent, reasoned explanation of one's beliefs.

gentleness and respect: This is not a call to disputation or argument about Christianity. Our attitude is most important if we are to be heard by others. We should not be contentious nor defensive.

may be ashamed: Those who slander the faith will see that what they say is untrue, because of the gentle and loving attitude of the Christians (in contrast to their own hostile attitudes).

slander: Gross distortions and rumors about Christianity abounded in the Roman world. For example, Christians were said to practice cannibalism (because they "received the body and blood of Jesus" in Holy Communion).

Comment

Is Christianity Rational?   *by Paul Little*

There are two equally erroneous viewpoints abroad today on the important question of whether Christianity is rational. The first is, in essence, an anti-intellectual approach to Christianity. Many misunderstand verses like Colossians 2:8: "See to it that no one makes a prey of you by philosophy and empty deceit, according to human tradition, according to the elemental spirits of the universe, and not according to Christ." Some use this verse in a way that gives the impression that Christianity is at least non-rational if not irrational. They fail to realize that a clearly reasoned presentation of the Gospel "is important—not as a rational substitute for faith, but as a ground for faith; not as a replacement for the Spirit's working but as a means by which the objective truth of God's Word can be made clear so that men will heed it as the vehicle of the Spirit, who convicts the world through its message."...

On the other hand there are those who think that becoming a Christian is an exclusively rational process. There is an intellectual factor in the Christian message, but there are also moral considerations. "If any man's will is to do his (God's) will, he shall know whether the teaching is from God or whether I (Jesus) am speaking of my own authority" (John 7:17). "The unspiritual man does not receive the gifts of the Spirit of God, for they are folly to him, and he is not able to understand them because they are spiritually discerned" (1 Corinthians 2:14). Apart from the work of the Holy Spirit, no man will believe. But one of the instruments the Holy Spirit uses to bring enlightenment is a reasonable explanation of the gospel and of God's dealings with men. It is quite true that an unenlightened mind cannot come to the truth of God unaided, but enlightenment brings comprehension of a rational body of truth....

The moral issue always overshadows the intellectual issue in Christianity. It is not that man cannot believe—it is that he "will not believe." Jesus pointed the Pharisees to this as the root of the problem. "You refuse to come to me," he told them, "that you may have life" (John 5:40). He makes it abundantly clear that moral commitment leads to a solution of the intellectual problem. "If any man's will is to do his will, he shall know whether the teaching is from God or whether I am speaking on my own authority" (John 7:17). Alleged intellectual problems are often a smoke screen covering moral rebellion.

A student once told me I had satisfactorily answered all his questions, "Are you going to become a Christian?" I asked.

"No," he replied.

Puzzled, I asked, "Why not?"

He admitted, "Frankly, because it would mess up the way I'm living." He realized that the real issue for him was not intellectual but moral.

The question is often asked, "If Christianity is rational and true, why is it that most educated people don't believe it?" The answer is simple. They don't believe it for the very same reason that most uneducated people don't believe it. They don't want to believe it. It's not a matter of brain power, for there are outstanding Christians in every field of the arts and sciences. It is primarily a matter of the will.[2]

The Art of Bible Study

Step Three: Personal Application

The final step in the application process is to apply what the text is saying to our own lives. Having understood how it applied to the original readers and how our situation parallels their situation, we are ready to listen to the text in the context of our own lives.

This is how Scripture changes us—by challenging us, by informing us, by bringing conviction to us, by encouraging us, by enlightening us, and by blessing us. But for this to happen, we have to approach the final step in the application process with the right attitude. We must stand humbly before the text, knowing it to be God's Word, and being open to what it says.

The first question we must ask is: What does this text say to me in the context of my life?

▶ What does it say to me as a citizen of the world, of a particular country, state, and town?

▶ What does it say to me as a member of a church?

▶ What does it say to me as a member of a family (as a husband, wife, parent, child)?

The second question we ask is the personal one:

▶ What does this text mean to me as a person seeking to follow Jesus?

This is often the only application question asked in Bible study and, since it is asked too quickly and without proper consideration, the responses are often too superficial. But once we have gone through all three steps in the application process, we are ready to ask the personal question.

How do we know we have heard the text correctly? We must ask ourselves:

▶ Am I challenged by what is said? If the text only (and always) serves to confirm what I already know, then I am not listening carefully enough. I have examined the text; now the text must examine me.

▶ Am I convicted by the Holy Spirit? Is there an inner sense of rightness to what is said, a challenge to grow and change, conviction of sin, and sense of being in the presence of God?

Extra Reading

The books that follow all deal with the reasons for the faith which we hold.

◆ *Know Why You Believe* (3rd ed.) by Paul Little (InterVarsity). Little answers the questions which university students typically ask.

◆ *Basic Christianity* by John Stott (InterVarsity). A superb outline of the reasons why Christians believe Christ to be God incarnate.

◆ *Mere Christianity* by C. S. Lewis (Macmillan). An extremely readable book, written from a different angle than the previous two.

◆ *Handbook of Christian Apologetics* by Peter Kreeft and Ronald Tacelli (InterVarsity). Two Boston College professors categorize, summarize, and offer compelling refutations of the major arguments against Christianity.

- *Christian Apologetics in a World Community* by William Dyrness (InterVarsity). A different approach to the defense of the faith.
- *Evidence That Demands a Verdict: Historical Evidences for the Christian Faith* compiled by Josh McDowell (Campus Crusade).
- *Understanding Jesus* by Alister McGrath (Zondervan). An Oxford scholar outlines the evidence for Jesus.
- *Who Was Jesus?* by N. T. Wright (Eerdmans). Another Oxford scholar responds to three recent books that portray Jesus in unorthodox ways.
- *I Believe in the Resurrection* by George Eldon Ladd (Eerdmans).
- *Who Moved the Stone?* by Frank Morison (Faber). Written by a lawyer who originally intended to produce a book disproving the Resurrection.
- *Easter Faith and History* by D. P. Fuller (Eerdmans). A scholarly study which examines the faith-vs.-history debate with new insights into the significance of Luke's accounts.
- *Miracles* by C. S. Lewis (Macmillan).
- *Are the New Testament Documents Reliable?* by F. F. Bruce (InterVarsity).
- *The Historical Reliability of the Gospels* by Craig Blomberg (InterVarsity).
- *The Problem of Pain* by C. S. Lewis (Macmillan).
- *Heaven: The Heart's Deepest Longing* by Peter Kreeft (Ignatius).

Reflection Questions

1. Think about the times when people have expressed resentment over the way you live. What was at the root of this resentment? Was there resentment because you sought to live out a Christian lifestyle? Was it because you were failing to live out a Christian lifestyle? Was the problem in you or in the other person (or group)?

2. Think about the times when there have been disagreements with your core beliefs. What was at the root of this disagreement? Was it because you were espousing Christian beliefs that were offensive for one reason or another? Or was it because of your failure to communicate your ideas properly? Were you harsh, dogmatic, unloving? Did you fail to listen? Was the problem in you or in the other person (or group)?

3. Where are the potential points of opposition to you as a Christian? In your family? At work? In your community? In your peer group? Among your friends? What is the issue? How can you work toward harmony in these situations?

4. How do you handle disagreement and opposition? Do you cave in? Stand firm? Change your beliefs and action to fit the group? Defend yourself? Give gentle and thoughtful reasons for who you are and what you believe?

5. Who can help you at times of attack? Where will you find encouragement and support? Who will give you straight talk to help you understand the dynamic of what is going on—both your part and the part of others?

---

[1] *First Epistle of Peter,* by A. M. Stibbs (Tyndale New Testament Commentaries, Grand Rapids: Eerdmans, 1969), page 55.

[2] *Know Why You Believe* by Paul E. Little (Downers Grove: InterVarsity, 1969), pages 1–2, 3, 4.

Journal

Chapter Six
Sharing Our Faith With Others

People may oppose us because of our faith. These days, however, opposition is the exception and not the rule. Generally, people are really interested in what we believe and why—especially in times of change. All over the world there is great upheaval: political systems are failing, economies are falling apart, new countries are being formed, tension between factions is growing, etc. And everyone is affected by this turmoil. In times of transition, people are open to new options. They want to know where hope, truth, and genuine security can be found. They want to know about Christianity.

The problem is that most of us are reluctant to talk about our faith. It is okay to do so in church among those who share our views. But with others, we don't know what to say: we fear a negative reaction; we are afraid of imposing our views on others. The list goes on for the reasons why we do not share the gospel.

Sharing our faith ought to be easy and natural. After all, the good news—that Jesus died to open the way to heaven and to make us into the kind of people we long to be—is the best kind of news. It's nothing to be shy about.

In this chapter, we will explore how to share our faith through a Bible study in which we meet a man who couldn't wait to share his experience of Jesus with others (Mark 5:1–20); through an essay in which Rosalind Rinker shares her experiences—good and bad—of sharing her faith; and by means of reflection on our own experiences of trying to share our faith.

The hope is that in the small group experience and through your own study, you will grow in your understanding of how to witness to others in a natural and convincing way.

Beginning *(20 minutes)*

Evangelists

Evangelists have acquired a bad reputation. This is unfortunate, because evangelism is a reputable New Testament concept. We need to recover the good name of evangelism through responsible faith-sharing.

1. When you see evangelists on television, how do you react?
   - ❏ Praise God!
   - ❏ What they say is true.
   - ❏ I don't understand what they are saying.
   - ❏ I want to respond.
   - ❏ Why do they keep asking for money?
   - ❏ Other: _____.
   - ❏ Forgive them, God!
   - ❏ I wish they wouldn't shout.
   - ❏ I guess they are sincere.
   - ❏ What are they trying to accomplish?
   - ❏ They are reaching some people.

2. Who shared his or her faith with you in a way that made sense? Describe the experience.

3. What's the most important thing you'd want to share about your faith? Why?

The Text

5 **They went across** the lake to the **region of the Gerasenes**. [2] When **Jesus got out of the boat**, **a man with an evil spirit** came from the **tombs** to meet him. [3]This man lived in the tombs, and **no one could bind him** any more, not even with a chain. [4]For he had often been chained hand and foot, but he tore the chains apart and broke the irons on his feet. No one was strong enough to subdue him. [5]Night and day among the tombs and in the hills he would **cry out** and **cut himself with stones**.

[6] When he saw Jesus from a distance, he ran and fell on his knees in front of him. [7]**He shouted** at the top of his voice, "What do you want with me, Jesus, Son of the Most High God? Swear to God that you won't torture me!" [8]For Jesus had said to him, "Come out of this man, you evil spirit!"

[9] Then Jesus asked him, **"What is your name?"**

"My name is **Legion**," he replied, "for we are many." [10]And he begged Jesus again and again not to send them out of the area.

[11]A large herd of pigs was feeding on the nearby hillside. [12]The demons begged Jesus, "**Send us among the pigs**; allow us to go into them." [13]He gave them permission, and the evil spirits came out and went into the pigs. The herd, about **two thousand** in number, rushed down the steep bank into the lake and were drowned.

[14] Those tending the pigs ran off and reported this in the town and countryside, and the people went out to see what had happened. [15]When they came to Jesus, they saw the man who had been possessed by the legion of demons, sitting there, **dressed and in his right mind**; and **they were afraid**. [16]Those who had seen it told the people what had happened to the demon-possessed man—and told about the pigs as well. [17]Then the people began to plead with Jesus to **leave their region**.

[18]As Jesus was getting into the boat, the man who had been demon-possessed **begged to go with him**. [19]Jesus did not let him, but said, "Go home to your family and **tell them** how much **the Lord** has done for you, and how he has had mercy on you." [20]So the man went away and began to **tell in the Decapolis** how much Jesus had done for him. And all the people were amazed.

Mark 5:1–20
New International Version

Understanding the Text (20 minutes)

We sometimes think we must go to seminary to learn how to share our faith. In this account, Jesus calls a man to be his witness who has had minimal (though powerful) experience of him, and little (or no) theological knowledge.

1. Identify the setting in which this incident occurred:
   ▶ Who are the various people mentioned here?
   ▶ Where did this take place?
   ▶ When did it take place (see Mark 4:1,35–41)?
   ▶ Try to visualize this setting. What do you see?

2. Describe the exorcism:
   ▶ What was the demon-possessed man like?
   ▶ What was going on in the dialogue between Jesus and the demoniac?
   ▶ What happened?

3. Describe the responses of the following people to this incident:
   ▶ the herdsmen   ▶ the townspeople
   ▶ the demoniac   ▶ the people of the Decapolis

4. What request was made of Jesus:
   ▶ by the townspeople? Why?
   ▶ by the demoniac? Why?

Optional Exercise

Imagine that you are a journalist. Write an account of this incident in your own words for the *Jerusalem Times*. Share your accounts with each other.

Applying the Text (20 minutes)

1. Consider the testimony of the demoniac to his family and to the people of the Decapolis:
   ▶ How would the ex-demoniac have described what the Lord had done for him?
   ▶ How might he have explained what happened to him?
   ▶ What might he have said about Jesus?
   ▶ What response might he have called for on the part of the people?

2. What is your testimony?[1]
   ▶ What has the Lord done for you?
   ▶ What can you say about Jesus?
   ▶ What response would you like your friends and family to make to Jesus?

3. What reactions to your testimony have you had (or might you expect):
   ▶ from your family?
   ▶ from friends?
   ▶ from people in general?

4. Which of the following will help to make faith-sharing a successful experience for you? Why?
   ❏ being natural
   ❏ being able to explain my experience
   ❏ knowing and using the right theological terms
   ❏ dialogue instead of monologue
   ❏ the right time and place
   ❏ being a good listener
   ❏ being genuine and honest
   ❏ other: _____

Optional Exercise

It is never easy to begin something new—like sharing your faith with others. But each venture must have a beginning. Plan together how each of you can begin to share your faith. Break up into sub-groups of four for this exercise.
   ▶ With whom will it be easiest for you to talk about your experience of Jesus? Make a list of people.
   ▶ When and where might it be appropriate to have such a conversation?
   ▶ What could you say to your friend?
   ▶ Try a role-play of sharing your faith. Let one person play your friend while you share your faith with them. Switch roles so each person has a practice run.
   ▶ End by sharing your lists with one another and praying together for a positive response from these friends.

Bible Study Notes

Setting: This is the second of four stories that Mark tells that demonstrate the awesome power of Jesus—power over the elements (4:35–41), here in this story, power over evil forces (5:1–20), power over chronic illness (5:24–34), and even power over death itself (5:21–23,35–43).

They went across: The disciples and Jesus started across the Sea of Galilee at dusk. They were then tossed around in a fierce storm and probably arrived on the other side in the middle of the night.

region of the Gerasenes: The exact location is uncertain, except that it was on the opposite shore from Capernaum (where they set off) in a Gentile region.

Jesus got out of the boat: No mention is made of the disciples. After their horrific experience in the storm (when they thought they were going to drown, and then the fright Jesus had given them by revealing that he had power to stop a storm), they were in no mood to set foot in a Gentile cemetery in the middle of the night where there was a madman (see 4:35–41).

a man with an evil spirit: The belief that evil spirits could possess and control people was widespread.

tombs: The ragged limestone cliffs along the shore were dotted with caves that were used as tombs. A graveyard at night was a place of great terror.

no one could bind him/cry out/cut himself with stones: The demoniac was a living nightmare—naked, impossibly strong, with cuts all over his body.

He shouted: A clash of wills begins as Jesus calls the demons forth from the man. In such a power conflict one person gained control over the other by knowing their true name (identity). So the demons cry out the true identity of Jesus: "Jesus, Son of the Most High God," but this fails to subdue Jesus.

"What is your name?": Jesus is much more powerful, and so he compels the demons to reveal themselves. The demons are named and cast out by the power of Jesus' name.

Legion: A company of 6,000 Roman soldiers who were, in the first century, the most powerful fighting force the world had ever known. "Legion" is an appropriate name for the overwhelming possession experienced by this man.

Send us among the pigs: It is not clear why the demons make this request, especially given the end result. Still, pigs (as unclean animals) are a more suitable home than a person for these evil creatures.

two thousand: So many pigs in one place probably means that this was the town herd, consisting of pigs owned by various people in the area.

dressed and in his right mind: When the townspeople return they find what they expected (drowned pigs), but also something they did not expect—a healed demoniac.

they were afraid: of the power of Jesus.

leave their region: He was probably seen by them as a powerful magician who posed a dire economic threat to the region.

begged to go with him: Not surprisingly the ex-demoniac wanted to leave this region (that held such awful memories for him) and these people (who had hounded him). His desire was to go with the man who healed him.

tell them: But Jesus leaves him as a witness to the community of what happened to him.

the Lord: This was an ambiguous title. It could mean "sir" or it could be a divine title (it is the name of God in the Greek OT). This is the only title that the ex-demoniac is given for Jesus—unless he could recall the name of Jesus that the demons had spoken through him.

tell in the Decapolis: He is, apparently, successful in his evangelism. The next time Jesus returns to the region (the name refers to a group of ten Gentile cities patterned after the Greek way of life), a large and eager crowd is waiting for him (Mark 7:31–8:10).

Comment

You Can Witness *by Rosalind Rinker*

People often give me this excuse for not sharing their faith verbally with others, "I can't express myself." Really? Then perhaps what you know and have experienced is on the meager side. Or perhaps you are under some false fear of what people may think of you? Or fear giving an incorrect answer? Or you may think people aren't interested? If so, all I can say is you don't understand people. Everyone carries some secret burden. Everyone longs for inner peace. Everyone wants a quiet heart. And everyone wants love and happiness.

Everyone is as stubborn about having religion thrust down his throat as you are! The human heart wants to make its own discoveries. But sometimes it wants someone who is an expert in gentleness to help. Certainly all of us resist anyone who claims to be an "authority" and who tells us what we must or must not do! We need freedom to believe! Freedom to live! We also need freedom to listen, to ask questions, to share and to search.

How can you share your faith then? This is a lifetime job, I admit. Finding ways and people, sharing and loving, hoping and praying.

First you must have a faith to share. Faith is the attitude we hold for a person we trust. "Have faith in God," Jesus taught His disciples. To be able to share, you must first know whom you believe. And what you believe. Sharing what you believe is witnessing.

Second, you must know how to witness with love. In order to share your faith, or to be a witness, you must not only experience God's love within yourself, you must open your heart. Then, like a river, this love will flow out of you.

"Perfect love casts out fear," wrote the apostle John. God's love can teach us—every step of the way—how truly to love others. All God requires is an open, receptive heart![2]

The Art of Bible Study

Application Exercises

Change is difficult. No one likes to change. To change is to admit we haven't been as faultless as we'd like to be. So we avoid changing. We dodge the challenges in the Bible. This is what makes application so hard for us.

This being the case, it is useful to do certain exercises that help us to see our need and to understand what the text is saying to us:

- *Newspaper:* Study a passage of Scripture and then read your daily newspaper. Go back to the text and ask yourself: what does this passage have to say concerning what I have just read?
- *Meditation:* Meditate on a passage after you have studied it. That is, mull it over in your mind, phrase by phrase. After each phrase ask yourself: what is this saying to me? (It is important to have studied the text thoroughly first, so you really know what it is saying.)
- *Prayer:* Pray over a passage. After you have studied, pray as follows: Begin by asking Jesus to be with you. Open yourself up to Jesus. Then discuss the passage with him. Go over it phrase by phrase, saying "Lord, what is it you want me to hear?" Pause often and listen.
- *Creative Imagination:* Try to visualize the passage in your imagination. If the passage is a story, watch the events unfold in your mind's eye. Visualize yourself in the situation. Listen to Jesus as he speaks to you. If it is a teaching section, listen to the author as he says this to a group of people which includes you. What impact does the passage have on you?
- *Journal:* Process the passage in your journal. Make notes as you consider what it means. Reflect on the passage as you write. Write out prayers that occur to you. Make resolutions about how to put it into practice.
- *Discuss:* Talk over the passage with a friend. Describe what it says. Ask your friend what he or she thinks it means, and what application it might have for you.

Extra Reading

There are many ways to do evangelism. The following books examine both the theory and the practice of outreach.

- *Out of the Salt Shaker & into the World: Evangelism as a Way of Life* by Rebecca Manley Pippert (InterVarsity). Evangelism in the context of relationships.
- *Tell the Truth: The Whole Gospel to the Whole Person by Whole People* by Will Metzger (InterVarsity). The process of God-centered evangelism.
- *Living Proof: Sharing the Gospel Naturally* by Jim Petersen (NavPress). Relational evangelism. There is also an excellent video series that can be used in a small group to learn these principles.
- *How to Share Your Faith Without Being Offensive* by Joyce Neville (Seabury). An Episcopalian laywoman talks about faith-sharing.
- *Explaining Your Faith Without Losing Your Friends* by Alister E. McGrath (Zondervan). The key concepts that we want to share with those who are not yet Christians: Jesus, the Resurrection, salvation, and God.

◆ *You Can Witness With Confidence* by Rosalind Rinker (Zondervan). One of the best introductory books on the subject of Christian witness. Sane, simple, interesting and practical, this is one book you ought to study thoroughly.

◆ *How to Give Away Your Faith* by Paul Little (Inter-Varsity). An amusing and perceptive study of witnessing, written by a man engaged in student evangelism.

◆ *Small Group Evangelism* by Richard Peace (InterVarsity. A multi-week training program to teach people how to do outreach through small groups.

◆ *Meeting Jesus* by James W. Sire (Harold Shaw) and *Introducing Jesus: Starting an Investigative Bible Study for Seekers* by Peter Scazzero (InterVarsity). Two sets of small group Bible studies for use with friends who want to know about Jesus.

◆ *Evangelism from the Bottom Up* by William Pannell (Zondervan). Evangelism that takes ethics and the urban reality seriously.

◆ *Reinventing Evangelism: New Strategies for Presenting Christ in Today's World* by Donald Posterski (InterVarsity). Evangelism that engages culture.

◆ *Reaching a New Generation: Strategies for Tomorrow's Church* by Alan J. Roxburgh (InterVarsity). Christian outreach that stresses community, ecology, and spirituality.

◆ *Christian Mission in the Modern World* by John R. W. Stott (InterVarsity). Lucid, thoughtful definitions and discussions of five key words: mission, evangelism, dialogue, salvation, and conversion.

◆ *The Master Plan of Salvation* by Robert E. Coleman (Revell).

Reflection Questions

Read the *Comment* section carefully and use it to assess your own attempts to share your faith:

▶ What excuses have you made for not witnessing? How valid are they?
▶ How would you want to be witnessed to? How can you be this way with others?
▶ What are the four or five main points of the faith you have to share?
▶ How can you witness with love?

Reflect on the whole process of witnessing. Read one of the books listed in the *Extra Reading* section to guide your reflection. Think about witnessing from the point of view of the other person. What would get through to that person? What language do you need to use? What attitudes should you exhibit? What communication skills are needed? What do you need to know about the gospel message?

If you skipped the *Optional Exercise* in *Applying the Text*, do it on your own using your *Journal*.

---

[1]A similar question was asked in chapter 6 of *Learning to Love Ourselves*. If you did that exercise, refer to it. This time, build upon what you said then.

[2]*You Can Witness With Confidence* by Rosalind Rinker (Grand Rapids: Zondervan Publishing House, 1962, 1969), pages 15–16, 36–37.

Journal

Chapter Seven
Serving Others

In the end, to love others means to serve others. This is, after all, the meaning of *agape* love: giving to others in response to their need without expecting anything in return. And indeed, the church down through the ages has been known as an agency of service. The church has built hospitals, established schools and universities, developed relief organizations, started farm co-ops, dug wells and latrines—and much, much more. All of this has been undertaken by Christians in response to Christ's call to love others.

Giving to others is not an optional exercise. In fact, it is the demonstration of our faith—as the text we will study indicates. It is not that we are saved through service but that service is the natural response of having been saved.

We will explore how to serve others through a Bible study in which James states in strong terms that faith produces good works (James 2:14–26); through two essays in which William Barclay sheds light on the supposed conflict between James and Paul and in which Elton Trueblood reminds the church that the important thing is not coming to church but going out from church to serve; and by means of reflection on three things: the form of service that most excites you, the meaning of the *LEARNING TO LOVE* course to you, and the process of journaling.

The hope is that through the small group experience and through your own study, you will grow in your understanding of how God is calling you to show his love to others by the way you serve.

Beginning (20 minutes)

Special Servants

Serving others takes place in many ways (big and small) and by many different people who embody the meaning of compassion.

1. Can you recall knowing, meeting, or reading about people who seemed to give themselves in a special way to others? Tell the group about one such person.
   - ❏ a parent who cared for children in difficult circumstances
   - ❏ someone who faithfully undertook a hard (or lowly) task for years
   - ❏ a nurse (doctor, teacher, etc.) who was especially caring
   - ❏ someone who gave a lot of time (money, effort) to a special project
   - ❏ a person who helped those who were less fortunate
   - ❏ a relative who willingly took care of a family member with a long-term illness
   - ❏ a highly skilled person who used those skills not for fame or fortune, but for others
   - ❏ someone whose ministry has been to the dying
   - ❏ other: _____

2. What did you learn from that person?

3. What would you like to be able to give to others?

The Text

¹⁴ What good is it, my brothers, if a man claims to have **faith** but has no **deeds**? Can **such faith** save him? ¹⁵**Suppose** a brother or sister is **without clothes and daily food**. ¹⁶If one of you says to him, "Go, I wish you well; keep warm and well fed," but does nothing about his physical needs, what good is it? ¹⁷In the same way, faith by itself, if it is not accompanied by action, is **dead**.

¹⁸**But someone will say,** "You have faith; I have deeds." **Show me your faith without deeds**, and I will show you my faith by what I do. ¹⁹**You believe that there is one God**. Good! Even the demons believe that—and shudder.

²⁰**You foolish man**, do you want evidence that faith without deeds is useless? ²¹Was not our ancestor **Abraham considered righteous for what he did** when he offered his son **Isaac on the altar**? ²²You see that **his faith and his actions were working together**, and his faith was made complete by what he did. ²³And the scripture was fulfilled that says, "Abraham believed God, and it was credited to him as righteousness," and he was called God's friend. ²⁴**You see that a person is justified by what he does and not by faith alone.**

²⁵In the same way, was not even **Rahab** the prostitute considered righteous for what she did when she gave lodging to the spies and sent them off in a different direction? ²⁶As the body without the spirit is dead, so faith without deeds is dead.

James 2:14–26
New International Version

Understanding the Text (20 minutes)

"He is so heavenly minded that he is no earthly good." Have you ever heard that? There is truth in this saying. Sometimes we are so concerned about our faith that we forget the world around us. This is not the way of Jesus, as James takes pains to point out in this passage.

1. Scan the passage in order to get a sense of James' argument:
   ▶ What two things are set in opposition to one another throughout the passage?
   ▶ What statement does James repeat four times (in various forms)?

2. Note the way James illustrates his main argument:
   ▶ What three illustrations does he use to demonstrate his main point?
   ▶ What is the point of each illustration?

3. One key to understanding James is understanding his definition of faith:
   ▶ What is the difference between faith and belief?
   ▶ What problem in the church might James be addressing?

4. Summarize what James is saying:
   ▶ What does he mean by "faith"?
   ▶ What does he mean by "deeds"?
   ▶ What is the connection between faith and deeds?
   ▶ Why is faith without deeds suspect?
   ▶ Why are deeds without faith suspect?

Optional Exercise

James uses three illustrations to show that faith is revealed by deeds. What other illustrations can you come up with to make the same point? Discuss how faith and deeds connect in the following situations:
- ◆ a village in Africa whose only water comes from a polluted stream
- ◆ the AIDS crisis in your community
- ◆ swastikas painted on the sides of Jewish temples
- ◆ other: _____

Applying the Text (20 minutes)

1. Compare what James says in verse 24 to what Paul says in Galatians 2:16: "...a man is not justified by works of the law but through faith in Jesus Christ.... because by the works of the law shall no one be justified."
   - ▶ In what ways do Paul and James seem to be teaching contradictory ideas?
   - ▶ How, in fact, do they actually complement rather than contradict each other?

2. What does James mean by the following "difficult" statements:
   - ▶ "Can such a faith save him" (verse 14); i.e., a faith without deeds? Yet we know it is by faith in Jesus we are saved, not by our good deeds.
   - ▶ "Faith by itself, if it is not accompanied by action, is dead" (verse 17). What is dead faith as opposed to a live faith?
   - ▶ "I will show you my faith by what I do" (verse 18). Can good deeds spring from no faith?
   - ▶ "His faith was made complete by what he [Abraham] did" (verse 22). Yet see verse 23 where his belief (faith) is noted.
   - ▶ "As the body without the spirit is dead, so faith without deeds is dead" (verse 26). What does this mean?

3. The challenge in this passage is not intellectual (understanding how faith and deeds connect) but practical.
   - ▶ What is the response of faith to the needs of people in verse 15?
   - ▶ What are we called to do in the face of the needs of others?

4. Based on what James says here, how should Christians respond in terms of time, money, and effort to the following areas of need:
   - ▶ hungry, homeless people   ▶ the sick
   - ▶ the uneducated, underemployed   ▶ the needs in other lands
   - ▶ unjust social structures   ▶ the need to share the gospel

5. Share with one another some of the ways you have responded to others in need.

Optional Exercise

Do the following case study: In a Midwestern city a new problem has arisen. There have been many divorces in the twenty to thirty-year-old age group. The result is that there are a growing number of young women with small children who have been left on their own. They are finding it extremely difficult to balance work (to make ends meet) and care of their children, keeping the home and car running (much less having any social life). A large church in this city has decided to reach out to this needy group. Plan a program that responds to the physical, economic, emotional, social, and spiritual needs of these young women.

Bible Study Notes

Setting: This section is part of a discussion of the poor and how to treat them. In the first part of the discussion (2:1–13), the issue is discrimination against the poor. Here the issue is charity toward the poor. This section is set in the context of a larger question: how do faith and works relate together? Incidentally, James (who wrote this epistle) is probably the brother of Jesus.

faith: The "faith" referred to here is not saving faith in the New Testament sense. It is mere belief or profession. In the New Testament, faith acts upon what is believed—e.g., a person believes in Jesus and so commits his or her life to Jesus. Mere intellectual acceptance is not enough. Faith without such trust is what James is talking about in verses 14–20; 24; and 26.

deeds: By "deeds" (or "works"), James has in mind ethical behavior.

such faith: The implication is that this is not real faith, and the implied answer to this rhetorical question is "No." Genuine faith reveals itself in good deeds.

Suppose: James offers a test case to prove his point (that to claim faith and fail to act in the face of need is an absurdity). Though this is only a hypothetical case, believers in Jerusalem were having a difficult time economically during the period in which James wrote. Many people lived on the edge of poverty.

without clothes and daily food: James chooses an extreme example. These are people who lack basic necessities. They will die without food or warmth.

dead: To assert that pious platitudes are enough is a sham. Such a person has no real faith.

But someone will say: James now responds to an imaginary opponent who raises a new issue: "Some people have faith, others have deeds. Both are the signs of religious people."

Show me your faith without deeds: James uses irony here. He does not believe genuine faith can exist without deeds. It is not, as his "opponent" asserts, an either/or situation; it is both/and. Faith is invisible— it only shows itself in deeds that reveal its presence.

You believe there is one God: This ringing declaration of monotheism, so unusual in first-century culture, was a belief that stood at the very heart of Judaism (and Christianity). James uses it as an example of belief that is inadequate. Merely believing this (as would everyone in the Judeo-Christian culture) is insufficient. Even the demons know that this is true. So it is not enough to be a cultural Christian.

You foolish man: The NIV obscures the harshness of the language here. This phrase is, literally, "You empty man." He is saying, "You fool."

Abraham: James concludes this section with two examples from the Old Testament, in which faith is demonstrated by actions.

considered righteous for what he did: Righteous action is evidence of genuine faith. In verse 23 he makes it clear that Abraham was acting from faith. It was his faith—not his action—that was credited to him as righteousness. The verse which is quoted (Genesis 15:6) comes when Abraham offered Isaac on the altar.

Isaac on the altar: This story is told in Genesis 22. God asks Abraham to sacrifice his only son, Isaac, as a burnt offering. Isaac's birth was itself a miracle, since both his parents were well beyond the years of child bearing. Isaac was Abraham's only hope that a great nation would come from him. To be willing to sacrifice him was a supreme act of faith. Abraham actually had the knife raised when God stopped him.

his faith and his actions were working together: This is what James urges: not faith alone or deeds without faith, but both working together. In this case, Abraham believed God's promise (verse 23) that he would raise up a great nation through him, and he acted on his belief by offering up his only son. His action demonstrated his faith.

You see that a person is justified by what he does and not by faith alone: This verse deeply distressed the great reformer Martin Luther, so much so that he called this book "an epistle of straw." But what James means is that intellectual faith alone is insufficient.

Rahab: The two spies that Joshua sent into Jericho were detected. They were saved by Rahab the harlot, who hid them from the king's soldiers. See Joshua 2 for Rahab's story.

Comment

Faith Versus Works　　　　　　　　　*by William Barclay*

The fact remains that James reads as if he were at variance with Paul; for…the main emphasis of Paul is upon grace and faith, and the main emphasis of James is upon action and works….

(First one must realize that) there are two kinds of belief. There is belief which is purely intellectual, and which consists in the acceptance of a fact with the mind. For instance, I believe that the square of a right-angled triangle equals the sum of the squares on the other two sides. I have no doubt that is true. If I had to, I could prove it—but it makes no difference at all to my life and my living. On the other hand, I believe that six and six make twelve, and, therefore, I will resolutely refuse to pay more than a shilling for two sixpenny bars of chocolate. I accept that fact—and I direct my life by it. What James is arguing against is, in fact, the first kind of belief, the acceptance of a fact without allowing the fact to have any influence upon life…. What, in fact, Paul held is the second kind of belief. To believe in Jesus was to take that belief into every part and section of life, and to live by it….

But, even allowing for that, there is still a difference between James and Paul. And the main difference is this—they begin at different times in the Christian life. Paul begins at the very beginning. He insists that no man can ever win or earn the forgiveness of God; no man can ever put himself into a right relationship with God. That initial step must come from the free grace of God…. James begins much later; James begins with the professing Christian, the man who already claims to have been forgiven, the man who already claims to be in this right relationship with God. Such a man, James rightly says, must live a new life for he is a new creature. He has been justified; he must now go on to show that he is sanctified. And with that Paul would have entirely agreed.[1]

A Coming in or a Going out Church?　　　　　*by Elton Trueblood*

The Church is never true to itself when it is living for itself, for if it is chiefly concerned with saving its own life, it will lose it. The nature of the Church is such that it must always be engaged in finding new ways by which to transcend itself. Its main responsibility is always outside its own walls in the redemption of common life. That is why we call it a redemptive society….

If this analysis is correct it bears closely on the question of what a Christian is meant to be in the twentieth century, as well as what Christians were in the first century. It means that no person is really a Christian at all unless he is an evangelist or is getting ready to be one. The person who supposes that he can be a Christian by observing a performance, whether of the Mass or anything else, has missed the whole idea. There is nothing wrong with watching a performance, providing the watching serves to make the daily apostleship more real, but there is terrible wrong in watching a performance whenever this serves as the end. The Church, however large its buildings and however grand its ceremonies or vestments, is a denial of Christ unless it is affecting the world—in business and government and education and many other segments of human experience.[2]

The Art of Bible Study

Making Applications

Hearing God's Word properly is the goal of Bible study. If we have been following the observation, interpretation, and application process carefully, we will be in a position to hear what God wants to say to us.

Here are some final thoughts on the application process:

◆ In the application process, what we are looking for is resonance: finding points of connection between the passage and our lives. In effect to "resonate" with a passage means, "Yes, that is true; that is me; I understand." It is a matter of spirit as much as intellect.

◆ We will never exhaust the Bible. Even if we have fully understood a passage (which is highly unlikely in most cases), our lives keep changing over time. So a passage connects with our situation in different ways at different times.

◆ Some passages are inherently richer than others. Certain passages move us, bless us, and challenge us at the core of our beings. Other passages—like the list of defeated kings in Joshua 12 or the details of different offerings in Leviticus 1–7—have little impact on us. They are still God's Word, but they have meaning in a different historical setting. Don't try to force application where there is none. Accept passages on their own terms.

◆ Don't lapse into allegorizing—making up meanings by asserting that this figure in the passage represents this idea, and so on. If you do this you can make the Bible almost anything and that is quite dangerous. There are a few passages in the Bible that are allegories, but the text will indicate when this is the case.

◆ Memorize key passages. In this way you can reflect on them during the day. Be sure, though, to study the verses as part of longer passages so that you do not misinterpret these verses by taking them out of context.

◆ The best way to hear what Scripture is saying to us is in a small group of others. We need each other to help us hear God's Word. We need others to help us put into practice what we hear. Accountability to one another is a scriptural concept.

◆ Be creative in working with application. The Bible is not dull; our study of the Bible should not be dull either. Use your God-given creativity to explore different ways to bring the text alive.

Extra Reading

These books deal with a variety of ways we as Christians serve others in the world we live in: social service, economics, justice, missions, racial relations, and the world of work.

◆ *A Passion for Jesus: A Passion for Justice* by Stephen Mott and Esther Bruland (Judson). A study guide for how to work for justice in this world. Highly recommended.

◆ *The Company of the Committed* by Elton Trueblood (Harper & Row). Trueblood suggests various ways in which the church can serve.

◆ *The Gospel People of Latin America* by Mike Berg and Paul Pretiz (MARC/LAM). Church growth in Latin America combines both spiritual and social renewal.

- *Redeeming the Routines: Bringing Theology to Life* by Robert Banks (Victor/ BridgePoint).
- *The Monday Connection: A Spirituality of Competence, Affirmation, and Support in the Workplace* by William Diehl (HarperCollins).
- *Freedom of Simplicity* by Richard Foster (Harper & Row).
- *Money Isn't God* by John White (InterVarsity).
- *Rich Christians in an Age of Hunger: A Biblical Study* by Ronald Sider (InterVarsity). Christian responsibility in the face of world hunger.
- *Completely Pro-life: Building a Consistent Stance on Abortion, the Family, Nuclear Weapons, and the Poor* by Ronald Sider (InterVarsity).
- *Counting the Cost: The Economics of Christian Stewardship* by Robin Klay (Eerdmans).
- *The Politics of Jesus* by John Howard Yoder (Eerdmans).
- *The Coming Race Wars? A Cry for Reconciliation* by William Pannell (Zondervan). A Christian perspective on what the L.A. riot of 1992 means.
- *More than Equals* by Spencer Perkins and Chris Rice (InterVarsity). A practical plan for racial reconciliation.
- *Christian Mission in the Modern World* by John R. W. Stott (InterVarsity).
- *Globaltrends* by Gordon Aeschliman (InterVarsity). Ten trends that will affect the world mission of the church.
- *Penetrating Missions' Final Frontier* by Tetsunao Yamamori (InterVarsity). Taking the gospel into politically or culturally closed nations.
- *Reaching the World Next Door* by Thom and Marcia Hopler (InterVarsity).
- *Romancing the Globe* by Dan Harrison and Gordon Aeschliman (InterVarsity). A new view of missions.

Reflection Questions

Use this final reflection exercise to think about not only this chapter, but the whole process of learning to love.

1. What forms of service excite your imagination? Helping the hungry, homeless, ill-clad, sick, uneducated? Political activism which creates social structures based on justice and governments that are well-run? Taking on social evils such as violence, poverty, racism, and economic exploitation? Getting involved in third-world countries? Missionary and evangelism work? Working with kids? Teaching survival skills? Education? Medical care? Working in prisons?
   ▶ In the past, what forms of service have you engaged in?
   ▶ At the moment, what kinds of service are you involved in?
   ▶ In the future, what kinds of service would you like to be involved with?

2. What are the major lessons you have learned from:
   ▶ *Learning to Love God?*
   ▶ *Learning to Love Ourselves?*
   ▶ *Learning to Love Others?*

3. Evaluate your experience of using a journal. How useful has this been for you? How can you make this a regular part of your life?
   ▶ You might wish to explore journaling by reading one of the following books on this topic: *Adventure Inward: Christian Growth Through*

Personal Journal Writing by Morton Kelsey (Augsburg, 1980); *How to Keep a Spiritual Journal* by Ronald Klug (Nelson, 1982); or *Keeping Your Personal Journal* by George F. Simons (Ballantine, 1978).

---

[1] *The Letters of James and Peter (The Daily Study Bible)*, translated and interpreted by William Barclay (Philadelphia: Westminster, 1958, 1960), pages 85–87.

[2] *The Company of the Committed* by Elton Trueblood (New York: Harper & Row, 1961), pages 69–71, 76–77.

Journal

The Art of Leadership
Brief Reflections on How to Lead a Small Group

It is not difficult to be a small group leader. All you need is:

◆ The willingness to do so;
◆ The commitment to read through all the materials prior to the session (including the leader's notes for that session);
◆ The sensitivity to others that will allow you to guide the discussion without dominating it;
◆ The willingness to have God use you as a small group leader.

Here are some basic small group principles that will help you to do your job.

Ask the questions: Your role is to ask the group to respond to each of the questions in the study guide. Simply read the questions and let various group members respond.

Guide the discussion: Ask follow-up questions (or make comments) that draw others into the discussion, and keep the discussion going. For example:
◆ "John, how would you answer the question?"
◆ "Anybody else have any insights into this question?"
◆ "Let's move on to the next question."

Start and stop on time: Your job is to start the group on time and (most importantly) to stop it on time. Certain people will always be late, so don't wait until they arrive. Make sure you end on time. If you don't, people will be hesitant to come again since they never know when they will get home.

Stick to the time allotted to each section: There is always more that can be said in response to any question. So if you do not stick very carefully to the time limits for each section, you will never finish the study. And this usually means the group will miss out on the very important application questions at the end of the session. It is your job to make sure that the discussion keeps moving from question to question. You may have to keep saying: "Well, it is time to move on to the next question." Remember: it is better to cut off discussion when it is going well than to let it go on until it dies out.

Model answers to questions: Whenever you ask a question to which everyone is expected to respond (for example, a *Beginning* question as opposed to a Bible study question), you, as leader, should be the first person to answer. In this way, you show others the right amount of time to respond. If you take 5 minutes to respond, everyone else in the group will feel that it is okay for them to take at least 5 minutes (so one question will take 50 minutes for the whole group to answer!). But if you take one minute to answer, so will everyone else (and the question takes only 10 minutes for the group to answer). Also, by responding first, you model an appropriate level of openness. Remember, the leader should be just a little bit more open than others.

Understand the intention of different kinds of questions: You will ask the group various kinds of questions. It is important for you to understand the purpose of each kind of question:

◆ *Experience questions:* These are often the first type of questions you will ask. The aim of these questions is to cause people to recall past experiences and share these memories with the group. There is no right or wrong answer to these questions. Such questions facilitate the group process by:
  • getting people to share their stories with one another.
  • being easy to answer, so everyone has something to say and thus the group conversation begins.
  • getting people to think about the session topic on the basis of their own experience.

◆ *Forced-choice questions:* Certain questions will be followed by a series of suggested answers (with check-boxes next to each possible answer). Generally, no particular answer is correct. In fact, often each answer is correct. By offering options, group members are aided in responding. This also helps direct the response. When people answer such questions, you may want to ask them to explain why they chose the answer they did.

◆ *Analysis questions:* These are questions that force the group to notice what the biblical text says and to probe it for meaning.

◆ *Application questions:* These questions help the group to make connections between the meaning of the text and each person's life circumstance.

◆ *Questions with multiple parts:* Sometimes a question is asked and then various aspects of it are listed below. Have the group answer each of the sub-questions. Their answers, taken together, will answer the initial question.

Introduce each section: It is your job to introduce each section. This may involve:
  ◆ *Overview:* Briefly explain the focus, purpose, and/or topic of the new section.
  ◆ *Instructions:* Explain how to do the exercise.

Comments: Occasionally it will be helpful to the group if you bring into the discussion some useful information that you have discovered from your own study. Never make long comments. Do not allow yourself to become the "expert" whom everyone turns to for "the right answer." Invite comments from others.

Some comments about how the small group discussion is structured in this book:

There are four parts to each small group session, and each has a different aim:

◆ *Beginning:* The purpose of this section is to:
  • Help people to move from the worries and concerns they brought with them (to the group) to the topic itself.
  • Start people thinking about the topic in terms of their own experiences.
  • Start discussion among group members.
  • Encourage people to tell their stories to each other so they get to know one another.

◆ *Reading the Text:* The purpose of this section is to:
  • Start the process of analyzing the text.
  • Let people hear what they will then study. Reading helps people to notice things in the text they might not see otherwise.
  • Focus on the text as the core of the small group study.

- *Understanding the Text:* The purpose of this section is to:
  - Immerse people in the text, so that they start to see what is there (the observation process).
  - Discern the main points of the text.
  - Understand the text as first-century hearers might have understood it.
- *Applying the Text:* The purpose of this section is to:
  - Understand what the text is saying (the interpretation process).
  - Apply the text to people's lives (the application process).

Begin each new session by:
- *Welcoming everyone.*
- *Opening in prayer:* Your prayer does not need to be long or complex. You can write it out beforehand. In your prayer, thank God for his presence. Ask him to guide the group into new wisdom, and to give each person the courage to respond to the text. You do not have to be the one who always opens in prayer. You can ask others to pray. It is usually a good idea to ask beforehand if a person is willing to pray aloud.
- *Introducing the topic:* Take no more than one minute to do this. Simply identify what you will be discussing, the text you will be studying, and the main ideas you will be examining. You will find this introductory material on the first page of each chapter.

Move to the *Beginning* exercise:
- Read the brief introduction aloud (when there is one), or just introduce the theme of the exercise.
- Give people a minute to read over the questions and think about their answers.
- Then as leader, begin the sharing by giving your answer to the first question:
  - Remember, there are no "right" answers—only personal stories or preferences.
  - Laughter is great medicine. These questions are seldom serious and invite funny stories (often from childhood).
- Move to the person on your right and ask him or her to respond.
- Go around the circle, so each person has a chance to respond to the question.
- Move to question two and do the same thing.
- Finish up with question three.
- Watch the time carefully so everyone has a chance to respond:
  - Don't worry if you do not complete all three questions, as long as people have started sharing.
  - After a few sessions, you will know how many questions you can complete with your group. You may need to pre-select one or two questions to use for this sharing time.
- Remember that even though this is lighthearted sharing, you are discussing the topic of the Bible study. Remind people of the theme of the session.

Move to the second section of the small group study—*Understanding the Text:*
- Introduce the Bible passage by reading aloud (or summarizing in your own words) the introduction to this section.
- Read the Bible passage (or invite someone else to read it).
- Give the group a few minutes to read over the passage, read through the questions (and think about the answers), and to consult the *Bible Study Notes*.

◆ Ask question 1:
  • Get responses from several people.
◆ When you feel that the question has been sufficiently discussed, move to the next question.
  • In this section, some of the initial questions are fact-oriented. There are specific answers to them. Subsequent questions will be more open-ended and will invite discussion.
◆ Work through all of the questions:
  • Be sure you have worked through the questions yourself beforehand, so that you know which are the important questions that need more time.
◆ If you still have time left for this section, use the optional question (where there is one). These invite a lot of discussion and personal sharing that will fill the remaining time.
  • You may decide to skip some questions and end with the *Optional Question* or *Exercise.*
◆ Remember: your aim in this section is to help the group notice what the text says and to begin to interpret it.

Move to the final section of the small group study—*Applying the Text:*
◆ Follow the same discussion process as the *Understanding the Text* section.
◆ Remember: your aim in this section is to help the group grasp the meaning of the text and to apply it to their lives.

Conclude the small group session:
◆ Discuss the *Personal Study* section for the coming week:
  • Encourage people to read over the *Bible Study Notes* (if they have not had time to do so during the small group).
  • Encourage the group to read the *Comment* section.
  • Encourage people to study and then work on the ideas in *The Art of Bible Study* section.
  • Encourage people to do *Journal* work.
◆ End with prayer together.

Serve coffee, tea, soft drinks, etc.:
◆ This will give people a chance to talk informally.
◆ There is often very good conversation following a small group session, as people hash over the evening's discussion.

Additional Exercises: There are a number of ways to enrich your small group session. You may want to add an extra exercise each week (e.g., start off each session with *Journal* sharing). Or you can vary the nature of the extra exercise (e.g., one week do a case study; the next week do a book report, etc.). What follows are suggestions for alternative or additional small group exercises.

Sub-Groups: You may want to divide the group into sub-groups of four for part of the sharing. This allows more time for each person to participate. Also, people who might be intimidated in a group of twelve find it easier to talk in a group of four.

- It is best to begin and end the session with everyone together.
- Do not form permanent sub-groups. Each week, have a different foursome meet together in a sub-group. In this way you maintain the identity of the whole group.

Journal: You may want to set aside time each week for people to share from their Journals. This can be a very powerful experience—you will discuss on a deep level the personal meaning of the previous week's passage.
- It is probably best to do this at the beginning of the session before you get into the new material.

Book Report: Bring along one (or more) of the books in the *Extra Reading* section:
- Discuss the content of the book.
- Ask someone else to discuss one of the books.

Comment: You may want to focus on the *Comment* section.
- Give people time to read it over (or read it aloud).
- Prepare questions that will enable the group to discuss the ideas in the *Comment* section.

Bible Study Notes: Some weeks you may want to spend time on these notes as a way of deepening the understanding of the text.
- You can do this by allowing more time for individual study of the text. Group members can then think about how they would answer each study question in light of the information in the notes.

The Art of Bible Study: It will be helpful to go over the process of Bible study from time to time—to encourage people to read and analyze the Bible on their own.
- Have someone report to the group about their experience in using some of these techniques.
- Make comments occasionally about *how* the group is analyzing the text at that moment. By doing this, you will highlight certain Bible study principles.

Sharing: Each week, ask a different person in the group to take five minutes and share how he or she came to faith. Or ask people to share how they applied biblical insights (from the previous study) to their lives during the week.

Case study: Tell the actual story of somebody you know (or read about) and then ask the group: How can the principles we have studied in this text help in this situation?

Small Group Leader's Guide
Notes on Each Session

If you are the small group leader, it is important for you to read carefully the section entitled *The Art of Leadership: Brief Reflections* on *How to Lead the Small Group*. This will help you in the general art of small group leadership. It will also provide you with ideas as to how you might tailor the material to fit the needs of your specific group. Then prior to each session, go over the notes for that session (see below). These notes focus on the specific materials in each session.

1

Overview
Potluck: Since this is the start of a new (though related) topic, some groups will be starting up for the first time; other groups will be re-starting after a break. If this is your situation, why not begin with a potluck supper together as a good way to launch this new venture. See the comments on *Session One* in the *Learning to Love God* book for some tips about how to do this.

Introduction
If your group is established already and has worked through *Learning to Love God* and *Learning to Love Ourselves* your introduction to the new book can be brief. Simply identify the theme of the next seven sessions and how each session connects to it. If this is a new group, make sure that you introduce the nature and direction of the small group. You will want to touch on:

▶ *Series Theme:* In the seven small group sessions, you will be discussing what it means to learn to love others. Thus you will be touching on various issues connected to human relationships. Your aim will be to clarify the biblical understanding of how we are meant to relate to one another. Read to the group the titles of each session to illustrate how this theme will be developed.

▶ *Group Process:* In each session, you will begin with a brief time of sharing (in which the topic is introduced by means of experiences group members have had). Then you will study together a passage from the Bible, using the questions in this study guide. These questions will help you come to grips with what the passage means and how it applies to your lives.

▶ *Group Details:* Describe where you will meet, when, and for how long.

▶ *Group Aims:* The hope is that group members will grow in their understanding of what it means to love others; that they will apply these insights to their lives; and that they will begin to understand how to study the Bible on their own.

▶ *Prayer:* Pray briefly, thanking God for assembling this group. Ask him to guide your deliberations and sharing today and during the coming weeks. Ask God to touch each life in such a way that the deep needs of that person are met.

Beginning

▶ *Questions 1 and 2:* Not everybody will have had especially warm relation-ships as a child. The feeling of not being loved is one of the problems of childhood. But try to avoid this issue (of not being loved), especially since this may be the first session for this particular group of people. Keep the conversation upbeat and positive. Everybody has somebody who has shown them love. Focus on positive experiences.

▶ *Question 3:* The list of traits is taken directly from 1 Corinthians 13, the passage you will study together as a group. Undoubtedly, people will want to name other traits that they consider foremost in a loving person (such as empathy, willingness to listen to you, warmth, etc.), but stick with this list. It will prepare the group to think about the passage. Incidentally, you can refer to this list of characteristics in your later dis-cussion (though they are not listed in the same order as in verses 4–7).

Understanding the Text

▶ *Question 1:* A good way to begin to understand a passage is to find the main point of a paragraph. The various suggestions by group members for paragraph titles will help people to see what Paul is trying to say.

▶ *Question 3:* Expect a lot of discussion about the definition of each charac-teristic of love. You may want to refer to a good dictionary or (even bet-ter) to William Barclay's commentary on 1 Corinthians (where he describes the original meaning of each word). Make sure the group has a good grasp of the nature of *agape* love.

▶ *Optional Exercise:* This is a paraphrase exercise. Sometimes when we put a passage into our own words, we understand it better.

Applying the Text

▶ *Question 1:* Discuss the way love works to give meaning to our activities in life. Discuss how we can act in certain ways on behalf of others, and yet have our actions tainted by a lack of love. Note, however, that others still benefit from what is done (e.g., the poor are genuinely aided).

▶ *Question 2:* This question will allow the group to personalize the charac-teristics of love. Remember that Paul describes a goal: none of us love perfectly, but this is what we should strive for.

▶ *Question 3:* There is a wide gap between knowing and doing. We can know what it means to be a loving person without becoming a loving person. Each of the issues listed can stand between the knowing and the doing. The aim of the discussion is to gain insight into how these problems function in real life. The second part of the question asks the group to move from the general (problems *people* have) to the specific (what *I* wrestle with).

▶ *Optional Question:* Discuss what it would mean if love were the operative principle in these various spheres. Be practical and specific. For example: "If we really loved each other in the church, we would rejoice when any-one had great success and help when anyone faced failure."

Concluding Issues

▶ *Group Covenant:* If this is the initial meeting of this group, have them turn to the section entitled: *How to Use It: Questions About the Study Guide.* Give the group a few minutes to look over the *Group Covenant.* Discuss the group ground rules. Make sure everyone is comfortable with these ground rules. End by going around the group and giving each person an opportunity to agree to the final group covenant.

▶ *Group Invitation:* If your first session is a "trial meeting," invite all who attended to return next week for chapter 2. Returning for the second week will signal that they are committed for the duration of the series (six more weeks). If you have room in the small group (i.e., there are less than twelve people), encourage group members to invite friends for the second session. After week two, no new members can join the group (since each time a new person comes, it is necessary to rebuild the sense of community).

▶ *Group Homework:* Some groups may ask members to prepare certain materials for the next session. If you decide to do this, go over the homework at this point. You might want to ask people to work through the *Comment* section and to put their observations in their journals. Or perhaps you ask each person to be prepared the following week to share one, brief *Journal* entry.

▶ *Group Prayer:* End with a time of prayer. Pray in a way that is comfortable for your group; i.e., you as leader lead in prayer, ask someone to pray, let various people pray briefly as led by God, etc., depending upon the group.

Other Materials

▶If this is the first session, it will probably be useful to the group for you to go over the *Study Resources* and *Personal Study* sections of the book so that everyone knows how these fit into the whole course.

- *Extra Reading:* Point out the variety of books that will allow further research on issues of interest.
- *Bible Study Notes:* Sometimes there is not enough time during the small group to do little more than glance at these notes. In that case, it would be useful for people to read them carefully on their own as a way of deepening their understanding of the text.
- *Comment:* The essays on self-love will provide more data for discussion. But if the *Comment* section is not used in the small group session, it can be studied during the week by each individual.
- *The Art of Bible Study:* A person who reads this carefully will (over the course of twenty-one sessions in three books) learn the rudiments of the inductive Bible study process. The hope is that these insights will enable people to study the Bible more profitably on their own. The focus in this book is on the application process in Bible study.
- *Reflection Questions:* These will guide personal reflection in the *Journal* section. They may also be used as small group discussion questions.

▶You may want to use some of this material as homework, which would be discussed in the next session.

Chapter Two

2

Introduction

▶ *Welcome:* Greet the small group and let them know how glad you are that they are all there. If this is a new small group, this means they have decided to be part of the group for the next six weeks. Tell them how much you are looking forward to your time together.

- *Prayer:* Pray briefly, thanking God for what he is doing in each person's life. Ask him to guide your deliberations and sharing today. Pray that during this session group members will come away with a new or deepened understanding of how families are meant to relate together.
- *Theme:* Refer people to the introduction to chapter 2 and the issue that will be discussed today.

Beginning

The first two questions are about the families you grew up in (not your present family if you are married).

▶ *Question 1:* Descriptions of our families can be great fun, given the wide range of people we are related to.

▶ *Question 2:* Share positive family memories.

▶ *Question 3:* Some in your group may not be married or currently live in a family environment, so take this into account in the discussion. Family traditions will often center around holidays or special days (like weddings, baptisms, or vacations).

Understanding the Text

▶ *Question 1:* This is an overview question in which the group notes the way various relationships are defined. Make sure they notice that all the relationships are controlled by the general guideline of mutual submission.

▶ *Question 2:* The issue of submission is one that needs discussion. Look carefully at what Paul says, and do not read into his words concepts that are not present. Note that the call for the wife to submit is simply a reiteration of the call for both husband and wife to be in a relationship of mutual submission. In other words, Paul does not say anything more to the wife. However, when he gets to the husband he has a lot to say!

▶ *Question 3:* In many ways, Paul's words to husbands are more demanding than what he says to wives.

Applying the Text

▶ *Questions 1, 2, and 3:* Think about how Paul's words apply to today's family.

▶ *Question 4:* Mutual submission is a hard concept to grasp, since it is not how we normally think of family relationships. Instead, we think in terms of hierarchy (in which there is almost a chain of command in the family). This is not Paul's view.

▶ *Question 5:* Getting family relationships right is hard work. Some of the dangers in missing the point are identified here.

▶ *Optional Discussion:* All cultures stand under the scrutiny of Scripture; all practices must be critiqued by Scripture. The difficulty is that sometimes it is very difficult to overcome our cultural assumptions. What Paul said was extremely radical in the first century. It is equally radical in many American homes. The reality of spouse and child abuse testifies to this fact. Try to hear what Paul has to say to our culture.

Other Materials

▶ The *Journal* reflections pose some interesting (and difficult) questions about our families. They may be used for group discussion, though some of this will be hard to discuss unless the group is very close.

Concluding Issues

▶ Assign homework (if any) and conclude in prayer together. In your prayer, thank God for the existence of families. Ask God to help you learn to love your family more and to learn from this relationship how to love others.

Chapter Three

3

Introduction

▶ *Prayer:* Pray briefly, thanking God for what he is doing in each person's life. Ask him to guide your deliberations and sharing today. Pray that during this session, God will help you to understand the nature of fellowship.

▶ *Theme:* Refer people to the introduction to chapter 3 and the issue that will be discussed today.

Beginning

▶ *Questions 1 and 2:* Some people are party animals; others are social hermits. Still, everyone prefers one type of gathering over other types. It should be a lot of fun to discuss these questions.

▶ *Question 3:* Remember what you learn here. You can use these ideas to plan your final small group party!

Understanding the Text

Since you are examining three separate texts, you will have to make sure to move quickly so that you have time to look at each text.

▶ *Question 1:* Do not forget that the aim here is to examine the nature of mutual love. The root question is: What is the nature of the love we should express to others in our Christian fellowship? You will ask this very question in the *Applying the Text* section.

▶ *Question 2:* Paul calls us to bear one another's burdens. We are not meant to carry them alone. We are meant to be there for each other.

▶ *Question 3:* The concept of unity is the focus here, with an additional reference to burden-bearing.

▶ *Optional Question:* We probably all have memories of especially good times of fellowship—moments when we felt connected together in Christ, loved and cared for, and energized by the experience. These experiences of fellowship come at different times in different ways: at a weekend retreat where there has been deep and honest sharing, in a small group that has grown to love one another, at times of crises in the church, during a powerful worship experience, etc. When fellowship prevails, the message of Christ becomes contagious and nearly irresistible (since the church is being what it is called to be). Remembering times of deep fellowship and identifying the dynamics at work at that time make it possible for us to be agents of fellowship by recreating those circumstances in our present situation.

Applying the Text

▶ *Question 1:* This series of questions moves from the meaning of mutual love (and its connection to fellowship) to the application of these concepts in the churches that group members attend.

▶ *Question 2:* These questions identify the nature of burden-sharing.

▶ *Question 3:* These questions wrestle with the connection between unity and fellowship, and how a certain way of life makes unity possible.

► *Optional Exercise:* This should be a fun and creative exercise in which the group throws out its best ideas for creating a fellowshiping church. Who knows how these ideas may then be carried out in the church that people are part of?

Concluding Issues

► Assign homework (if any) and conclude in prayer together. Pray that each person will know and experience the explosive power of Christian fellowship. Pray that each person will know what he or she should do to create, foster, and sustain fellowship in his or her church.

Chapter Four

4

Introduction

► *Prayer:* Pray briefly, thanking God for what he is doing in each person's life. Ask God to guide your deliberations and sharing today. Pray that during this session the group will develop a clear understanding of the Christian lifestyle.

► *Theme:* Refer people to the introduction to chapter 4 and the issue that will be discussed today.

Beginning

► *Question 1:* The group will probably be able to add a number of other taboos that they remember from their childhood.

► *Questions 2 and 3:* Having a list of forbidden behaviors is one thing; following that list is another.

Understanding the Text

► *Questions 1, 2, and 3:* These questions will guide you through an examination of the chapter by focusing on each of the paragraphs. In particular, you will look for general principles that help us to stay in fellowship with those who have different views about what Christians should or should not do. Note that what is in view here is behavior which sincere Christians disagree about—not behavior which the NT is clear on. Such things as lying, cheating, stealing, committing adultery, and murder are not matters of conscience. They are forbidden!

► *Optional Exercise:* Paraphrasing is a good way to make sure you understand what is being said. If you can't put Paul's ideas into your own words, you probably haven't fully understood what Paul is saying. You may want to divide the group into sub-groups of four for this exercise so that everyone has the opportunity to read his or her paraphrase.

Applying the Text

► *Question 1:* This question gets to the heart of the matter. The issues listed are matters over which Christians disagree—sometimes to the point of breaking off fellowship with those who feel differently.

► *Question 2:* The first question probed what some Christians choose not to do as a matter of religious practice. This question considers what some Christians choose to do as a matter of religious conviction. The choice isn't binding on every Christian in either case. And personal choices shouldn't lead Christians to disdain or judge others who have chosen differently.

▶ *Question 3:* The focus in this passage is not on different lifestyle choices, but on how to get along with people who hold different convictions. Explore this issue using this series of questions. A new issue is introduced here: the matter of distinguishing between those who are "weak" in faith (and constrained in matters of lifestyle) and those who are "pharisaical" in faith (and seek to bind others to their law). The first type of person is the subject of this passage. Paul deals with second type, the "Judaizers" (who would re-introduce the law into Christianity), in his letter to the Galatians.

▶ *Optional Exercise:* Try to save time for this final exercise. It will generate interesting and useful discussion that should clarify what Paul is saying.

Concluding Issues

▶ Assign homework (if any) and conclude in prayer together. Pray that each person will gain new insight into how to handle differences within the Christian community.

Chapter Five

5 Introduction

▶ *Prayer:* Pray briefly, thanking God for what he is doing in each person's life. Asking God to guide your deliberations and sharing today.

▶ *Theme:* Refer people to the introduction to chapter 5 and the issue that will be discussed today.

Beginning

▶ *Question 1:* Group members will probably be able to remember many other topics they argued about as kids.

▶ *Questions 2 and 3:* Different kids (and adults) respond in different ways to controversy. You will probably be surprised at the diversity in the group. It is good to be aware of the ways we handle controversy.

Understanding the Text

▶ *Question 1:* Peter urges Christians to live in such a way as to promote harmony. This is the first line of defense against persecution.

▶ *Question 2:* Peter then discusses persecution—how to avoid it and how to meet it.

▶ *Question 3:* Now Peter alludes to another form of persecution: opposition for what Christians believe. This is different from the opposition for how Christians live; i.e., for "doing what is right."

▶ *Optional Exercise:* The group may or may not be able to respond to these questions (which are typical of what people ask). You should aim for two results from this exercise: (1) that people will learn new "facts of the faith" from one another, and be better equipped to discuss these issues with others; and (2) that people will be motivated to find out how to respond (there are good responses to each question). Encourage group members to acquire and study the books by John Stott and Paul Little. These books are a good start in mastering the "reasons for our faith."

Applying the Text
▶ *Question 1:* These questions explore how to promote harmony with others. Christians should be active (and not passive) when it comes to promoting peace.

▶ *Question 2:* But we cannot always avoid harassment. In fact, sometimes it is our Christian behavior to which people take exception. In each of the illustrations, the assumption is that these folks are obeying Peter's commands; i.e., they seek harmony.

▶ *Question 3:* Remember the nature of these scenarios: behavior that masquerades as Christian but is, in fact, inappropriate. The young man who shares the gospel may have good intentions, but his manner (being aggressive, not listening to others, finger-pointing judgment, anger when people do not believe, lack of courtesy, refusal to take "No" for an answer) is so offensive that his relatives cannot hear his words (which are true). The problem with the clerk is that she has no right to insist that others follow a code of behavior they do not necessarily support, so she is seen as self-righteous.

▶ *Question 4:* In a culture that is so pluralistic, Christian beliefs are bound to be offensive to some. We need to understand why people might take exception to what we believe, and we should be ready with a gentle and thoughtful response to the questions we are asked.

▶ *Optional Exercise:* It is important to distinguish between genuine opposition (which is rare in North America) and opposition which is brought on by our own less-than-Christian attitudes to others. It is not that we want to push people away; sometimes we don't realize how we come across to others. So it is not the good news that brings a reaction, but our insensitive behavior! Don't give the impression in this discussion that all Christians are always feisty and hard to get along with. This should be seen as a caution not to display negative attitudes—not an indictment of everyone.

Concluding Issues
▶ Assign homework (if any) and conclude in prayer together. Pray that each person will gain new insight into how to handle opposition.

Chapter Six

Introduction
▶ *Prayer:* Pray briefly, thanking God for what he is doing in each person's life. Ask God to guide your deliberations and sharing today.

▶ *Theme:* Refer people to the introduction to chapter 6 and the issue that will be discussed today.

Beginning
▶ *Question 1:* You probably need to explain that not all evangelists are the same. There are many sincere, reputable men and women who communicate the good news about Jesus. But unfortunately there are other evangelists who are not so reputable, and they give everyone else a bad name.

▶ *Question 2:* Most of us come to faith through the witness of someone else. The sharing of good experiences of evangelism will balance off the bad examples we see on television.

▶ *Question 3:* We are also called to be evangelists. What is at the heart of what we want to share?

Understanding the Text

▶ *Question 1:* You are reading a narrative passage, so it is important to get the setting clearly in mind. Ask one or two people to describe in their own words what this setting must have been like. This was a really spooky situation, like a nightmare or horror film.

▶ *Question 2:* The exorcism consisted of a power battle between the force of good (Jesus) and the force of evil (the demons). In this, each seeks to gain dominance over the other by invoking the true name (identity) of the other. See the *Bible Study Notes* for more details. Notice how the name of Jesus prevails over evil in its most powerful form.

▶ *Question 3:* The herdsmen were the original "witnesses" in this account, the first to tell the story of what happened. The townspeople, being Gentiles, did not know about Jesus and could only assume he was a powerful wizard. They feared him because Jesus believed that the life of one shattered man was worth more than their whole herd. The demoniac was restored and became an effective witness, one whose testimony astonished the Greek-speaking people of the Decapolis.

▶ *Optional Exercise:* This is a great opportunity for a paraphrase. It will force people to put all the details into an account, along with explanations of what happened. You may want to split into sub-groups of four so each person is able to read his paraphrase.

Applying the Text

▶ *Question 1:* The aim here is to recreate the testimony of the ex-demoniac. Remember, it would not be very sophisticated (since he only spent a short time with Jesus), and it would not have had any theological background.

▶ *Question 2:* The aim here, of course, is for each person to think about his or her testimony. If the group did the testimony exercise in chapter 6 of *Learning to Love Ourselves,* you can build on that experience.

▶ *Question 3:* Most people have tried to share their faith, not always with good results. If you have time, you might want to analyze the various experiences group members have had.

▶ *Question 4:* Obviously some of the items on this list will help in sharing the faith, while others will hinder it. After you discuss the positive points, you might go back and discuss why the other items would work against a good experience.

▶ *Optional Exercise:* Give people support as they do this exercise, since sharing the faith is sometimes a bit frightening. Emphasize that this is about conversation, not monologue (where they might lecture their friends). The more natural the conversation is, the better, and the same gentle attitudes discussed in the last chapter should prevail.

Concluding Issues

▶ Assign homework (if any) and conclude in prayer together. Pray that each person will gain new insight into how to share his or her faith with others.

Chapter Seven

7   *Introduction*
   ▶ *Prayer:* Pray briefly, thanking God for what he is doing in each person's life. Ask God to guide your deliberations and sharing today.
   ▶ *Theme:* Refer people to the introduction to chapter 7 and the issue that will be discussed today.

Beginning
   ▶ *Question 1:* Such people don't need to be people we know personally (though it is best if this is the case). If all else fails, people can bring up Mother Teresa!
   ▶ *Question 2:* Meeting people like this is always challenging. We are inspired. We see new options. We learn in many ways from such people.
   ▶ *Question 3:* We come away with a desire to be better people ourselves: more patient, more loving, more selfless, more giving. They set high standards for us.

Understanding the Text
   ▶ *Question 1:* With some passages, it's best to begin by scanning them to get a sense of the main argument.
   ▶ *Question 2:* This is a highly visual passage. James wants his readers to see what he is saying. The hungry, poorly-clad illustration is clear: true faith provides food and clothing. The Abraham illustration is more complex, since it presupposes a knowledge of the original incident (as well as knowledge of the nature of justification). Still, the point is clear: in the dramatic case of Abraham and Isaac, faith (deep trust in God) and deeds (the willingness to undertake an extreme act) went hand in hand. Abraham would not have acted as he did without faith. Rahab acted as she did because she believed that the God of Israel had given the land into his people's hands.
   ▶ *Question 3:* The difference between intellectual belief and trusting faith is key to James' argument. It would seem that a kind of nominal faith had arisen in his church, where people professed belief in Christ but this made little difference in the way they lived.
   ▶ *Question 4:* This question asks the group to express the point of the passage. Note, however, that James only deals with faith that has no deeds. He does not address deeds without faith—but since this is an issue in our secular society, ask the group to think about deeds without faith.
   ▶ *Optional Exercise:* Each of the examples ask us to respond to needs of people who may or may not have any connection to the church.

Applying the Text
   ▶ *Questions 1 and 2:* The first two questions probe the seeming contradiction between what Paul says ("justification is by faith alone" and what James says "faith without works is dead"). In fact, this is not a genuine contradiction when James is rightly understood. In *Question One,* the basic resolution is developed. Then in *Question 2,* it is used to make sense out of the difficult parts of the passage.
   ▶ *Question 3:* Lest the group be sidetracked into an intellectual discussion (which would distress James!), this question gets back to the core issue.
   ▶ *Question 4:* This general discussion will help the group to think about

various ways in which people can serve. However, be sure to make the point that one person cannot respond to every need. God calls us to certain needs. The point is not that we must respond to every need (who can?), but that our faith does result in action on behalf of others. This is the meaning of *agape* love.

▶ *Question 5:* Seeing what people are doing by way of service is always rewarding. Our acts don't need to be dramatic (selling our house in the suburbs and living with the homeless in the city). Giving to charities, helping to raise money for Africa at the church fair, and working with the Little League are all part of giving. If a person insists he or she is doing nothing (which is highly unlikely), then have them talk about what they hope to do in the future.

▶ *Optional Exercise:* The extent to which you can consider this issue will be limited by the time available. But take into account the rather complex set of issues around this need. There are matters of child care (can the church help here?), social needs (perhaps the church can create a group), emotional needs (a support group?), justice issues (how can the fathers be part of the solution?); economic needs (a job bank?), and spiritual needs (how can these women be drawn into the life of the church?).

Farewell Party

Since this is the final session not only in this book, but also for the *LEARNING TO LOVE* series, plan a farewell party to recall what the small group meant to each person. You can also use this time to plan the next small group series, and to give everyone a chance to say goodbye. During this time you can:

◆ *Share memories:* Ask group members to recall the best moments in the group, as well as the worst moments! What did they appreciate about the group? What did they learn?

◆ *Plan the next series of small group sessions:* You may want to take week or two break before you begin again. Or you may need to take a longer break if Christmas, summer, or some other special time is coming. Or you may just wish to continue meeting weekly. Explore what next you can study together. It may be time to study a particular NT book together. Or study a particular topic that is of interest to everyone.

• Decide whether to keep group membership the same or to invite new members. Some group members may not be able to attend the new series. Bid them farewell. Think about how you can recruit new members. Or you may decide that one or two of your group will form a new group to go through *Learning to Love God* or *Learning to Love Ourselves* again with new people.

• Decide how the next group will be led.

Have a Party!

Arrange for the kind of food and drink that will produce a good celebration. Enjoy each other. After all, a party is all about being with friends in a relaxed atmosphere—and you have made new friends during these seven weeks (and have deepened old friendships).

Epilogue:
A Summary of the Series

"A new command I give you: Love one another. As I have loved you, so you must love one another. By this all men will know that you are my disciples, if you love one another" (John 13:34-35).

It all comes down to love. This is the heart of the Christian life: To love God and be loved by him. To love others and so reveal God's love. To love yourself properly and so be able to love others.

To learn to love is a lifelong process. We never get it fully right, but we do grow in our ability to love and to be loved. In these studies we have touched upon the various elements of love.

To love God we must know God. And knowing God involves encountering him (so he is no longer an idea but a reality), giving our lives to him (by repentance and faith in Jesus), and then resting in the assurance that he has accepted us (not because of what we have done, but because of what Jesus has accomplished on our behalf). But we cannot rest on a past experience, no matter how dramatic; nor can we be content with growing up in the faith and always knowing God. We must enter into the way of faith (a path well-trod by saints before us) in which we reach out to God in prayer (to enter into conversation with him), in Bible study (to listen to his revealed truth and will), and in worship (to join together with the vast company of others who worship him).

But we must also pay attention to who we are as we walk after God. It is Jesus who bids us to love ourselves properly. And in order to do this, we must know who we really are: men and women created in the image of God (a little lower than the angels) yet flawed and fallen (never able to do it right or be right in a perfect way). Yet we are called to strive for righteousness: to live a life in which our behavior reflects our commitment to Jesus, to depend upon the ready forgiveness of God when we fall, to forget what is past and striving with gusto into the future of God's heavenward call, to seek all the while to be who we are: men and women made to participate in the very life of God.

All this—our endeavor to love God and love ourselves properly—is made known to the world around us by our love of others. We begin by loving our families—the people nearest and dearest to us. We seek also to love our new family (our brothers and sisters in Christ) in the reality of fellowship that so invigorates and motivates us. We work to make peace with those in this fellowship who see things differently (knowing that we all serve the same Lord). From this secure base (the love of our families and the love of our community) we reach out beyond this circle to those who do not yet know Christ—despite the opposition we sometimes experience. We share our faith with them and serve them in the name of Christ.

It is in this service that the love of God and the love of self in Christ is made known. Our faith is revealed by our deeds. Ours is no secret faith, expressed only in the mysteries of the Temple, and revealed to the company of the committed. It is shown in the cup of cold water given in Jesus' name (Matthew 10:42), in the food and clothing provided to those who have none (James 2:14-17). And so our love comes full circle. We love God and are loved by God. In Christ we come to love ourselves and are therefore able to love others. And in loving others, we reveal our love for God.

Learning to love is a lifelong pilgrimage. It is this pilgrimage that brings the kind of growth that moves us steadily toward what we long to be—men and women who are fully ourselves, made in the image of God, standing in the presence of God, and receiving that highest of all commendations: "Well done, thou good and faithful servant" (Matthew 25:21).

May God bless you as you walk this pilgrim way of love.

SMALL-GROUP MATERIALS FROM NAVPRESS

BIBLE STUDY SERIES

DESIGN FOR DISCIPLESHIP
GOD IN YOU
GOD'S DESIGN FOR THE FAMILY
INSTITUTE OF BIBLICAL
 COUNSELING Series
LEARNING TO LOVE Series

LIFECHANGE
RADICAL RELATIONSHIPS
SPIRITUAL DISCIPLINES
STUDIES IN CHRISTIAN LIVING
THINKING THROUGH DISCIPLESHIP

TOPICAL BIBLE STUDIES

Becoming a Woman of Excellence
Becoming a Woman of Freedom
Becoming a Woman of Prayer
Becoming a Woman of Purpose
The Blessing Study Guide
Homemaking
Intimacy with God
Loving Your Husband

Loving Your Wife
A Mother's Legacy
Praying From God's Heart
Surviving Life in the Fast Lane
To Run and Not Grow Tired
To Walk and Not Grow Weary
What God Does When Men Pray
When the Squeeze Is On

BIBLE STUDIES WITH COMPANION BOOKS

Bold Love
Daughters of Eve
The Discipline of Grace
The Feminine Journey
Inside Out
The Masculine Journey
The Practice of Godliness
The Pursuit of Holiness

Secret Longings of the Heart
Spiritual Disciplines
Tame Your Fears
Transforming Grace
Trusting God
What Makes a Man?
The Wounded Heart

RESOURCES

Brothers!
Discipleship Journal's Best
 Small-Group Ideas
How to Build a Small Groups Ministry
How to Lead Small Groups
Jesus Cares for Women
The Navigator Bible Studies
 Handbook

The Small Group Leaders
 Training Course
Topical Memory System
 (KJV/NIV and NASB/NKJV)
Topical Memory System:
 Life Issues